From HOLY HOUR To HAPPY HOUR

From Holy Hour To Happy Hour

How to Build Christian Community

Francis X. Gaeta

Resurrection Press
Mineola • New York

Other titles by the author:

From Ashes to Fire: A Companion for Our Forty Days of Feasting and Fasting

What Shall I Give Him, Poor as I Am? Reflections for Advent and Christmastide

Copies may be purchased from St. Brigid Parish, Westbury, NY 11590
(516) 334-0021

"Spirit of Christmas" (p. 125), original artwork by Father Edward Hays, 1995. Color prints available from Forest Peace Publishing, Inc., 251 Muncie, Leavenworth, KS 66048.

First published in October 1996 by Resurrection Press, Ltd.
P.O. Box 248
Williston Park, NY 11596

ISBN 1-878718-34-7

Library of Congress Catalog Card Number 96-68372

Cover design by John Murello

Cover photo by Ken Spencer; Copyright 1995, Newsday, Inc.

Inside photos by Ken Spencer

Printed in the United States of America.

This book is dedicated in loving memory
of
Fr. Frederick F. Schaefer
Pastor of St. Brigid's from 1975 to 1989
Received into eternal life on August 20, 1996
who laid the foundations and gave the vision
for all that followed

and in loving gratitude to the Staff of St. Brigid's
whose love, dedication and giftedness
allow it all to happen...

Deacon Robert P. Broyles, Deacon William F. Byrne, Paul and Stephanie Clagnaz, Rev. Thomas C. Costa, Rev. Claude J. D'Souza, Deacon John D. Falls, Marie Firenze, Jennifer Gallagher, Mary Grossi, Ted Henderson, Rev. Martin Klein, Christine Lombardi, Sr. Judith Mannix, RGS, Robert Martella, Deacon Felix J. Matheis, Adriana Miller, Deacon James P. Morris, Sr. Marie Patrick McDermott, SSND, Estelle Peck, Susan Porteus and Mary Jane Witte, and also in loving memory of Tommy Ciotti Thorell.

From the bottom of my heart I thank you for all that you have done to make St. Brigid's a family and for making it such a joy to go from "holy hour to happy hour."

Special thanks are due to Emilie Cerar of Resurrection Press and Estelle Peck of St. Brigid's for their patient and painstaking editing of the manuscript. Without them this book would never have become a reality.

Contents

Foreword

By his hugs you shall know him. The hugs that Msgr. Francis X. Gaeta dispenses are not timid, pro-forma hugs, holding you at a safe distance. They are enthusiastic, industrial-strength, bear-wrestling, count-all-your-ribs-when-he's-finished hugs. If hugging were an Olympic event, he would be wearing gold.

But the hugs are not just an interesting personality quirk. They are essential to his whole vision of parish. "People will not join or stay in the Church because of some great theological insight," Father Frank writes. "They will be hugged into the Church and they will stay if they find God there."

This book is a hug in print. It begins with Father Frank's theology of community, then offers practical ideas for building a parish that hugs people, that rocks them safely in the divine embrace and keeps them there.

"The Church should be the greatest toucher and hugger," he writes. "The Church should be the greatest lover of all."

But that is easier said than done. Every Catholic has spent time in parishes that don't hug so much as shrug. They are cool, distant, efficient dispensers of grace. They are, as Father Frank calls them, filling stations. Step right up, get your high-test grace. See you next week: same time, same place.

That is not the way St. Brigid's works. It pulls people in with warm welcome and lively liturgy, with humor and amazing energy.

If you are looking for a filling station where you can pick up your grace dispassionately, without the messy necessity of reaching out to others, without hugging, hand-shaking and loud amens, then this is not the place for you.

If you prefer a parish where a monsignor is really a monsignor, where the associate pastors would not dare to poke fun at the pastor in public and mock the long, loving way that he drawls out the word "be-yoooo-tee-full," then you are looking for a more traditional church, the kind I call St. Rigid's — not St. Brigid's.

The style of the pastor has a lot to do with setting the tone. Clearly, St. Brigid's believes in a community of disciples, in which lay people share ministry with the ordained. But just as clearly, the pastor is the leader, and the parish reflects his style and his philosophy.

Do not be fooled. On the surface, Father Frank's approach to pastoring looks as simple as a hug. One of his priests once joked that Father Frank's theology is much like a cake, "sweet and syrupy, with no substance." But that was a joke. The truth is, he has thought out what he's about, and his approach to pastoring reflects a greater depth of theology than appears on the surface.

In fact, priests who know him well describe Father Frank as "a pastoral genius." This implies no esoteric formulae, but a simple reality: When it comes to liturgy and parish life, he does not think in terms of either/or, but both/and. "Frank would say, 'If it leads you to God, let's do it,'" says Manuel Ramos, a leader of the Hispanic community at St. Brigid's.

In other words, in a parish with a rich variety of people, Father Frank believes in offering an equally rich menu of spiritual experiences. "We try to create as many opportunities as possible, on a quasi-sacramental basis, to lead people into some kind of touching of God," Father Frank says.

His pastoral style flows from his deep sense of the sacramental, of the presence of God in the everyday lives of ordinary people — in the eating, the drinking, the singing, the weeping, the birthing, the marrying, the burying.

"Our holiness is in the ordinary," he told a baptism preparation class. "Our holiness is in loving with everything we've got, and in loving the way Jesus loved. The church doesn't make me holy. The church doesn't make you holy. The church reminds us of what we already possess."

That is his theology in a nutshell, and the first part of this book explains it at greater length and with more nuance. In the second part of the book, Father Frank gets down to business, explaining the way St. Brigid's works and sharing his ideas for liturgy, for ministry, for parish life.

His ideas, like his hugs, are robust and plentiful. Focusing on that lavish flow of ideas, one of his parishioners, Anne Josey, whose distinctively enthusiastic "Amen!" at liturgies is a parish trademark, has dubbed him "Father Brainstorm."

Those ideas, along with the ideas of his staff and of the parishioners, form the core of the parish's unique style. But ideas do no good if they stay with the originator. One of Father Frank's often-repeated concerns is that pastors don't do enough to share ideas with one another. They don't find the time to sit down together over some pasta and wine and tell each other what ideas work, so that the good ideas will help people in parishes far removed from the one where they started. The second part of this book is Father Frank's way of sharing the ideas of St. Brigid's with other parishes.

If this book is gentle and welcoming in outlining its ideas, that is simply the style of the parish. A quick example: Some priests feel uncomfortable at weddings, which throw them together with the "unchurched," who are there for the wedding but don't regularly appear at parish liturgies. And when some priests look out in the pews at Christmas or Easter and see so many unfamiliar faces looking back, they can't resist saying something critical from the pulpit. But that attitude fails to take into account the nature of a church that Jesus launched with words about seeking out the stray sheep. "The spirit of love and welcome has to fill the church — no wisecracks about not seeing them 'til next Easter allowed!" Father Frank writes.

If this book is joyful, that is a reflection of Father Frank's attitude toward his vocation. He clearly loves being a priest. "Priesthood, to me, is relationship; I could never live without that," he once told me. "It has to be in relationship to people. Honestly, the depth of love between priest and people and friends, it's a beautiful, beautiful thing."

Finally, if this book is collaborative, conveying a broad vision of lay responsibility for the life of the parish, that is because Father Frank believes it. Though other priests have called him a pastoral genius, he writes: "Over the years I've learned that many people know much more than I do and that they can do things better than I can. If I'm not threatened by that, then I can have hundreds of people working with me and I come up looking like a genius!"

As the fruit of the collective genius of St. Brigid's parish, this book can go a long way toward helping you bring some of what is valuable and life-giving in the spirit of St. Brigid's to your own parish community. Take it to heart.

Bob Keeler

Introduction

"From Holy Hour To Happy Hour" has become a mantra at St. Brigid's since Fr. Joe Nagle first coined it. It does in a way summarize an understanding of what sacrament and community are in the life of our parish. It speaks of how a relationship with Jesus builds on a relationship with the community and vice versa. It also speaks of how a parish must work to build these relationships.

This book is intended for everyone who is involved in parish life and ministry. It is not meant exclusively for priests, sisters, deacons and lay professionals, although they should find it especially helpful. The principles described in this book really apply to everyone. By baptism we are all shepherds/pastors. Each of us is responsible for part of the flock of Christ.

In the building of Christian community we cannot abdicate responsibility by allowing the hierarchy or the clergy and religious to have all the power. They don't. Every one of us has power to create the part of the Body of Christ in which we are active.

We all build or destroy community. Many seem to have an unhealthy clerical mentality that still sees the clergy as the real Church with the real power. I hope that this book will help each one of us claim our true power with the realization that claiming power demands the paying of the price needed to build our community, our life and our love.

In this book I will also offer some very practical advice on just how to go about building this community. We will go through the liturgical year and the calendar year and suggest some tried and true ways to build the spirit of community, service, love and fun among God's people. The practical approach will comprise Part II of the book.

Part I of the book will establish the spirituality and theology upon which Part II is built. The practical ways of celebrating community are limited only by our sense of adventure and creativity. Suggestions made from practices at St. Brigid's will only be a springboard to other creative interpretations that you can try in your own parish community.

Part I is the key. There is a very real spirituality of parish leadership based on the model of the life of Jesus — the Paschal Mystery. While it is a joyful way of life, it does demand a very serious commitment. Part I will invite the pastoral team to deeply reflect on their love and commitment to their community. While Part II is wide open in terms of what a particular community will do to implement its theology and spirituality, Part I is not.

Part I will challenge a community to reflect on why it exists in the first place! The reason why many parishes are not exciting and not alive is that Part I exists only in theory and not in practice. Until it is actualized a parish can go nowhere.

I believe that it is very helpful to listen and "pick the brains" of colleagues. What is working for them? What stirs the excitement for God in *their* hearts? I never leave a group of people without some new thoughts of how I can change, add to, or enhance the ministries in St. Brigid's.

If you are not a very creative person you are in good company. Most of us are not. I have had very few original ideas, but I am very quick to act upon something that I think will work. I am a complete eclectic. I have no profound theological or liturgical principles. My bottom line always is: Will it bring people closer to Jesus? Will it help them? If so, let's do it!

Recently I had dinner with a great priest, Fr. Jim McDonald, who told me about a Mass he celebrates on the feast of St. Gerard Majella for couples who are trying to conceive. Because of his suggestion we began such a Mass this year here at St. Brigid's. We pray over and anoint these couples and bless them with St. Gerard's relic. We make it a beautiful night of prayer and celebration. Why do we do it? We do it because of the pain and struggles of so many couples who yearn for a child and the need of the parish to love them and pray with them. They are family. They are in pain and they need our love and support.

So, in St. Brigid's we stand on the shoulders of the priests, sisters, lay staff and deacons who are there now and who served in the past. But many people and institutions influence us. The candles at the end of the pews at Christmas and Easter are the inspiration of St. Thomas Episcopal Church in New York, the prayer line "Moment with Jesus" is inspired by Fr. Denis Kelleher, the Presepio by the Metropolitan Museum of Art and St. Anthony's Church in "Beautiful Rocky Point" — the list goes on and on.

One of the great tragedies of the Church is that there are so few vehicles for the sharing of ideas. Think what we have to offer each other! That's why I write this book: to share what has worked in one faith community.

Part III of this book is a sampling of some of the promotion we do in the weekly parish bulletin (nineteen pages each week) and in other local papers. Advertising is evangelization and vice versa. We will speak a lot about that and give some very practical examples which we use at St. Brigid's. So, get ready! Pray through Part I, laugh through Part II and roll up your sleeves for Part III! I pray that in this little book you will find many sound, good and workable ideas and be motivated to add to them. Let's have a ball! Look who we're working for!

I thank you for the privilege of sharing the life of one parish, *my* parish, *my* beloved family, with you. I pray with you that our hearts will be open to the Holy Spirit and that we will work together to build communities where Jesus is allowed to truly live. I pray that our beloved Mother Mary will keep our little flocks in her loving protection.

In Jesus' love,
Francis X. Gaeta

Part One

The Faith and Spirituality of Parish Life

Chapter One

A Community of Love

With all my heart and soul I believe that the Church is the Body of Christ. I also believe that the Church is the family of God and that I am bound to every man, woman and child on this planet because of the Incarnation of Jesus Christ. I believe that in Christ I am part of everyone and that they are part of me. I believe that this relationship in the Spirit is as real and as profound as the bond of flesh and blood. I believe that I am truly part of the Body of Christ. But just believing all these beautiful things about the Church is not enough. If they are to have the influence on my life that they are meant to have, I must also experience what it means to be part of the Body of Christ. Knowing and believing are just not good enough.

A Developing Sense of Church

I received a fine education from the seminary in the late fifties and early sixties. Courses in Pauline theology and ecclesiology helped me to construct my personal vision of what Church was all about. The encyclicals of Pius XII, teachings of theologians on the Body of Christ and developments in the liturgical movement helped me to solidify a theology of Church and ministry that was primarily relational and co-responsible with all the people of God. The excesses of clericalism were already on the way out. We were thinking about and trying to live Church very much in the spirit of *Gaudium et Spes* and *Lumen Gentium* before they had been written. This was possible because their genius was being taught unofficially and sometimes clandestinely long before they were "baptized" by Vatican II.

My theology of Church has certainly deepened since the sixties, but it was pretty much in place at my ordination in 1963. I knew the theology, read the scriptures and celebrated the liturgy of a Church that was formed by the death and resurrection of the Lord Jesus. This Church called me into relationship with the Lord and with all my sisters and brothers. Love and service were to be the very heart and hallmark of this mystery we called Church. I knew all the "right" words, believed them with all my heart, but never really felt or experienced what Church meant — not until I made a Cursillo in January of 1965. The Cursillo made real everything I had read and studied about the Church. For the first time I experienced Christian community.

Before the Cursillo, my spirituality and prayer were completely personal. The Cursillo opened my eyes to see that spirituality and prayer are always both personal and communal. I never come to the Lord all alone. It is always with sisters and brothers. My pre-Cursillo spirituality saw holiness as basically a fleeing from the world to find God. After the Cursillo I realized that although I deeply need the private and contemplative aspects of my life, I cannot truly touch the Holy One without touching people. The Cursillo forced me to see that what I often considered unimportant or secondary really was the most important. It is an extraordinary adventure to discover in true Ignatian style that God truly is present in all things. That discovery is still being fleshed out in my life.

Holiness in Relationship

My Cursillo experience — call it an "explosion" — has compelled me over the years to see everything in a new way and with a new heart. Family and friendships have taken on a totally different meaning for me. Relationship is where I primarily find the Lord. My own quest for holiness is to live all the relationships of my life as completely and as lovingly as I can. *The priesthood for me means to belong to my people and to allow them to belong to me.* I see my life as one in which I am called to share my life with sisters and brothers as they become "flesh of my flesh and bone of my bone."

The only thing that truly touches us is the knowledge that we are loved. The "successful" or "effective" priest touches his people not because of his theology, style or personal gifts. He touches his people only when he loves them and allows them to love him. The successful parish is the place where God's people experience this love — priests, sisters, deacons and lay staff loving others and being loved in return.

What Community Is

Community is the place where I feel loved, accepted, important and known. Community is not just the place where I am told about the love that God has for me in Christ Jesus; it is the place where *I* am loved and empowered by that community to give that love to other people. Community is far more than correct theological, scriptural and moral teaching. If the doctrines of the Church do not personally engage and touch me, I can never really hear them or respond to them.

People don't understand and accept Catholic teaching because of logical and scientific explanations, as true and as correct as they may be. Somehow these truths must come alive. The only place where this happens today is in a living and vibrant community that is always in the process of celebrating the sacrament of friendship and family. Every group and every parish needs the "explosion" of a Cursillo-type experience if it is going to become a real community and pass from mere formal adherence to principle and rule to a living and joyful sharing of faith and life.

New Life in the Spirit

So many wonderful movements have sprung up in the last thirty years to provide a means of going beyond mere cerebral acceptance of dogmas and moral laws to embracing a new life in the Holy Spirit lived in the loving embrace of a true family. Movements such as the Cursillo, Marriage Encounter, Renew, At Home Retreats, Genesis II, Romans VIII, Engaged Encounter, Life In the Spirit Seminar, Retrouvaille—just to name a few—have one thing in common: They create a Christian community where the meaning of love, discipleship and friendship take on totally new dimensions.

These special programs (sometimes celebrated outside the parish) have to be part of the normal parish life. *The building of community is the first task for the parish, its leadership and all its members*. All the works of the Gospel to which we are committed as a parish will not prosper except in the context of Christian community.

The Right to Exist

Until people's hearts are touched, they are unlikely to be interested enough to listen or respond to the Message. Community is not a gimmick to help evangelization. Community *is* evangelization. The Gospel that we preach is that all people are loved. When this love is experienced, then the Message has a chance to be heard. When we are not loved, then the Church is perceived as a self-serving salvation machine more interested in controlling people and collecting money than in serving them.

For the Gospel to be heard, everything in a parish must be done as an act of love. Everything must be done to put flesh and blood on the Gospel of Love and Salvation. Every liturgy, program, activity and ministry a parish is engaged in must be a way for Jesus, the Loving and Forgiving One, to touch and embrace His people.

When a parish is perceived chiefly as a business or a place that is impersonal, cold, disinterested, unfeeling and "out of it," then it becomes almost impossible to preach the Gospel with power and to truly touch people. *When the parish becomes the sacrament of the welcoming, loving and forgiving Jesus then everything is taken care of — even the finances.* When a parish does not do this, we begin to question the very meaning of parish, even to the point of asking if a parish has the right to exist.

A Parish Family

These are hard words. The days of the "filling station" parish are over. Our people want and demand more than just the "administration" of the sacraments. They look more and more for a Church and a community where God personally touches and speaks to them through the love and friendship of a new family — their parish family. *People don't leave the Church because they don't believe what the Church teaches but because there is no personal and compelling reason to remain.*

What is the Church saying that impacts on the real issues — the meaning of life, love, sickness, death and the future? Are there people who will walk with me on my journey? Will someone be by my side as I face the evils of AIDS or cancer?

All the right answers, all the perfect liturgies, all the best courses in Scripture will mean nothing to me unless I am personally loved in my parish and unless I know that I belong to something much greater than I can ever be by myself. I must *experience* being a part of the Body of Christ.

Once I have my "explosion" or "breakthrough," then I can give to others what I have received myself. I can be the Body of Christ because I have been touched, loved, forgiven, and empowered by that Body of Christ.

On the Mount of the Transfiguration, Peter, James and John had an experience of Jesus that they could never forget for the rest of their lives. Even in the dark and terrible moments of their lives they could think back to that moment of glory when they saw their Jesus as He truly was — the Son of Man and the Son of God. It's the same way with community — once you've experienced it, once you've seen Jesus in His Church as He truly is, you can never forget it and you can never be content until your parish becomes the family that Jesus wants it to be.

Chapter Two

The Home of God

The people of God want their parish to be a community. They want it to reflect all the wonderful aspects of family. They want it to be a place where one is known, accepted, loved, supported and at times challenged. They want the parish to be more than just a place to dispense spiritual blessings. The big question is: Are we willing to *pay the price* necessary for a parish to become and remain a community? This is the key question.

A Covenant of Love

Parishes don't become communities because they are wealthy or because they contain very talented or even holy people. They do not become communities simply because they have gifted or charismatic leadership. Certainly, all these things help, but of themselves they will not achieve what we're looking for. *A parish becomes a community when the leaders are willing to enter into the Paschal Mystery and live and die for their people.* It is only in this embracing of the Paschal Mystery that the new life of resurrection is able to come forth. This new life is community. It is family.

Entering the Paschal Mystery means that one has a covenant of love with one's parish. It means loving people with one's heart and soul. It means that the parish is the life of the shepherd. It means that it is clear to everyone that the leader of the community is in love with his people and is delighted to be with them. It means *really* living with one's people. It means being part of all they are and all they experience. It means being the Good Shepherd and laying down one's life for one's flock. It also means being a sheep and allowing one's family to minister to and to love one back.

Love One Another

There are many parishes where everything is "right" according to the book, but everything is wrong in terms of touching people and really making them feel at home. Make no mistake about it, it's wonderful to have beautiful buildings and manicured lawns. It's great to have money and a large and talented staff. It is a joy to have beautiful music and extensive programs. But all of this doesn't make it a community unless the leadership has said to everyone, "I love you and I give you permission to love me and to love one another."

This "price" for community is very real. This "price" we speak about is what the leadership is willing to give to the parish, namely: relationship, affection, presence and commitment. (*We will look at each of these in detail later in the book.*)

In the Gospel of John (*Jn 15:17*), Jesus insists that His disciples must "love one another as I have loved you." The model of the love of the shepherd is none other than that of Jesus himself. How does Jesus love us? He loves us to the point of laying down His life on the cross for us. He gives everything and holds back nothing. His gift is Himself. He gives all that He is and all that He possesses.

In order for a parish to begin to become a community, the pastor must obviously love the people. It is not enough that the people see their pastor as a good man, a fine preacher, gifted administrator or devout celebrant. They have to see him as one who really loves *them,* who is giving his life for the flock, and who is happy, fulfilled and joyful being with them and living his life as a part of theirs.

What is said of the pastor is also said of the associate pastors, the religious sisters, the deacons and the lay staff. All of these ministers must be perceived as people who are working together to build up the Body of Christ and as people who truly love their work and the sisters and brothers they serve.

A self-giving love — to the point of dying for the beloved — is the only love that will ever make community possible. It is in the joy and peace of this loving that the seeds of new life are planted — seeds that will renew the earth and the Church. This new life will endure forever. One will confidently seek new ways to be sure that new life is always forthcoming within oneself, one's family and one's parish.

Community is more than people getting along or feeling good about themselves. Community is more than achieving success in programs and projects. Community is more than fine buildings and money in the bank. Community is the birth of a new creation in Jesus Christ, in which one discovers who one truly is and is accepted and loved for that. *Community is where I am formed, healed, forgiven, inspired and empowered.* Once one has experienced community, one cannot settle for anything less.

There will never be community if the clergy and parish staff come across as middle management bureaucrats. We may say all the right things about community, bonding, family and all the other "in" things, but the proof of the pudding comes when someone makes a phone call to the parish or CCD office. If you are treated poorly, all the right words from the pulpit or in the bulletin will mean little. The message will come across loud and clear, "These people really don't care about me. They're running a business."

Creating the Vision

In the present structure of the Catholic Church, the pastor holds most of the cards of power. He makes the parish agenda. The pastor creates the tone of the parish. Eventually the staff will reflect his personality and vision of Church. If the pastor is willing and delighted to pay the price for community, the staff will usually follow his lead.

The price for community is very high. We all get tired. We are all tempted to throw in the towel. We all fail. We need to be constantly refreshed and renewed. Prayer and reflection are not luxuries; they are necessities. The process of paying the price for community is really an ongoing quest for Jesus in prayer and in the mutual support of our sisters and brothers.

The staff must be given great latitude and encouragement to use their gifts and to love the people. Doing so confirms the "permission" to love one another. If the pastor is not willing or able to pay the price for community, individual staff members can become the "real" pastors, by loving their people and creating the atmosphere for trust and growth in a parish.

Pockets of Hope

There are parishes where the CCD or Parish Outreach Office becomes the "real" parish. They become the place where the people are welcomed and loved unconditionally. They are the fun places where all the excitement and the ideas generate. They are the places where people learn that *they* are the Church and share the love of Christ. They are the places where real prayer takes place in the parish. These pockets of hope in the parish exist because there is an associate pastor, a sister, a deacon or a lay person who knows what it costs to build community and is delighted and happy to "pay" the price to be the good shepherd. Others follow their lead and they wait for the conversion or the replacement of the pastor.

Qualities of a Pastor

The appointment of pastors is a serious responsibility of the bishop of the diocese. Men cannot be made pastors because they are good administrators, good fund-raisers, good preachers or even good celebrants of the liturgy. All of these qualities are wonderful and the Lord will use them powerfully for the building up of the Body. But the most important questions to consider in appointing a pastor are: Is he a lover? Will he gladly pay the price of building community? Will he be a loving father/brother to his family?

We can ask it in another way, "Is his life motivated by the spirit of the fruits of the Holy Spirit found in Galatians 5? Is he truly a man of love, joy, peace, patience, goodness, fidelity, gentleness and self-control?" When these forces are operative in the life of a man, he has the major qualifications needed to be a shepherd of souls. While other gifts are very useful and necessary, they build on to these qualities found in Galatians 5 and they are never a substitute for them.

If the leader of a parish has as his main passion the love of God and people, communities will form. If the leader is more comfortable being an administrator, much good can happen, but the parish will never become what the Lord wishes it to be: a home, a family and a community.

Whose Are You?

Every pastor and priest, every sister and deacon, every lay minister must be in the process of ongoing conversion. We must always remember what Sr. Thea Bowman asked the bishops of the United States: "Who are you?" and "Whose are you?" If we expect our people to be connected, if we expect them to "let go" and enter into the mystery of Jesus, his death and resurrection, how can we do less? How can we expect anything less of ourselves?

When a pastor or other leader knows, understands and accepts this role as the chief lover, all the other gifts needed to guide and run the Church will come forth from the Body of Christ. Christ-centered leadership calls forth and welcomes all the sisters and brothers and the gifts they have to give to the Body. It is not only OK, it is *expected* that there will be many who are smarter and more gifted than the leader. There will also be many who are holier and closer to the

Lord. What matters is that the leaders be willing to lay down their lives for their community and that they become a real part of the community.

Passionate Celibacy

There is so much today written about the politics of celibacy. The only meaning that celibacy has is that priests or sisters passionately love their God and their people and are totally free to be committed to them. They must *belong* to their people. They must become "flesh of my flesh" and "bone of my bone." Celibacy has much less to do with sexual activity than it does with belonging and loving. Celibacy without passion for one's people degenerates into the oil of efficiency to keep the cogs of the machine running smoothly. *Passionate celibacy empowers, inspires, encourages and challenges everyone to live the Gospel and to love more completely.* The happy and loving celibate is the greatest gift to the community. In today's Church there are often more married and single "celibates" than there are celibate "celibates." These people are teaching the celibates how to be celibate by the powerful example of the evangelical way in which they live their married and single lives. We must allow the Holy Spirit to teach us by the example of one another.

Parents Build Community

Perhaps no one pays the price of building community more than loving parents raising their children. When a father and mother, or a single parent literally lay down their lives in love for their beloved children, family life truly happens. Is there any love as close to the love of God as that of parents? Parents are so filled with the love of God that there is nothing they will not do for their children. It is in the giving of oneself for the beloved that the Paschal Mystery is experienced and in that love community is formed and nurtured.

The Rewards of Community

While we have to be realistic about the cost of building community, we can never underestimate the rewards. When you are really into it, there's just nothing like it! The laying down of one's life is not really burdensome or painful. It is a joy. There is nothing that equals the satisfaction and joy of serving the Lord and truly being part of a family. The love and the affirmation that the loving and dedicated parish minister receives more than compensates for the "cost" one pays for building that community. It is truly in the laying down of one's life in love and joy that one receives the hundred fold that Jesus promises.

In the process we acquire a wealth, a love, a joy and a reward that this world cannot give. It is the treasure of knowing the love of God in Christ Jesus the Lord and sharing that love with countless sisters and brothers. The more this love is shared, the more the love grows and the deeper the bonds of community and family become.

When the good shepherds love their flocks, they send out a message that says it is OK to love yourself and one another. Permission is given to love. That permission is given in parishes, homes and organizations. When it is accepted and believed, the revolution begins and the Body of Christ is born again. *The Church becomes the home of God instead of the house of God!*

Chapter Three

The Sanctity of Relationship

We have all grown to appreciate that our spirituality is relational. Holiness has less to do with doing good things than it does with belonging to and cherishing the beloved. Whether it is friendship, marriage, parenthood or priesthood, what really matters and what really transforms is the depth of the relationship — the doing, caring, forgiving and challenging — that are part of every true relationship.

The "price" of community is paid over and over again as the leadership is committed to forming and maintaining the relationship of love between itself and the people. As this relationship grows it gives the community itself "permission" to grow in love and relationship with one another. This relationship has certain characteristics without which there can never be real bonding in Christ's love.

Real community is based on love. The Gospel imperative of Jesus constantly comes to mind, "Love one another as I have loved you" (*Jn 15:12*). The pastoral leadership and all parish ministers need to be reminded that to qualify for a leadership position one must take these words of Jesus very seriously. To assume this role one must know that he/she is called literally to laying down one's life for the flock — the People of God. There has to be a very conscious decision made every day to love one's people as Christ first loved them. Everything the shepherd does is meant to be an expression of love and service to the family, just as everything a husband and wife do is an act of love. Marriage Encounter speaks so eloquently about making a decision to love each day. More than a feeling or emotion, it is a dedication of one's life to the love of the Paschal Mystery in which Jesus gives His life for His beloved spouse, the Church.

A Place Where Everyone Is Loved

Where does this love come from? It is a gift of the Holy Spirit. It must be begged for in prayer and it must be worked on every single day. It means an embracing of all of God's people including the unattractive, the difficult and the troublesome. It is not just seeking out the likable, or the rich and the gifted. A parish that is in the process of becoming a family is the place where all kinds of people feel loved. They feel loved because they *are* loved; they are made to feel welcome and important because they *are* important.

There are groups in every parish that sense they are not important or even wanted. Whenever I put something in the parish bulletin that lovingly welcomes homosexuals, I always receive letters thanking me. Frequently the letter writers will say that the piece in the bulletin was the first time that they were ever acknowledged, let alone made to feel welcome. "Could it be that the Church loves me, too?" they say.

I have had the same kind of response when I acknowledge in a positive way the ministry and the holiness of single parents, the divorced and single persons. When they feel that they are loved and important, they blossom and share with the Church the richness of their spirituality and love.

Calling Others to Love

To say that I love my people is one of the most life-changing statements I will ever make. It means that my whole life is set in a new direction. It means that a given community then becomes the focus of my life. It means that all of my gifts and talents are theirs (along with the concomitant weaknesses and faults). It means living out the words that I lead others so often in pronouncing—"for better or worse, for richer or poorer, in sickness and in health until death."

It is this kind of love that the priests, sisters, deacons, lay staff and parish ministers are called to have for their people. The ministers, lay staff and deacons will also bring to this covenant the richness of their sacraments of marriage and parenthood. As the leadership makes this kind of commitment of love to their family, the family picks it up very quickly and begins to live it and share it among themselves. As the leadership says, "I love you," and means it, great things begin to happen in the family. Love is experienced and love begins to be shared and the Christian community is born.

Parishes today find it impossible to satisfy all the needs of their people. Shortages of clergy and women religious make the job even tougher. The Church and parish leaders need to ask themselves: Is it my job to satisfy all the needs of my parish or is it my job to help create a community of love where the people themselves will fulfill these needs? Where there is a true community of love, ministries flourish. People come forth to do everything from gardening to bringing Communion to the sick. They *want* to be a part of a family. When they are encouraged to love one another and when friendship and love flourish, every need will be satisfied and every ministry will be fulfilled. It is in the relationship of love and community that the Church comes alive and all that is needed — from talent to money — will come forth in abundance.

It becomes clearer each day that my main job as pastor is to be a lover. If I do that and call others to love, "giving them permission," then the work of the Lord will be done powerfully and beautifully.

Chapter Four

Embracing One Another

Love: Showing Affection

Love must be expressed or it dies. Anyone in the helping professions has repeatedly heard the complaints: He never told me that he loved me. She never held me. He never kissed me. How many good people have waited until death to let another know what was in their heart?

We have all read and heard so much about dysfunctional families. A parish in which affection is not experienced is dysfunctional. It doesn't matter what it preaches about affection. If you don't communicate to me in *some* way that you love me, I don't know it. The same is true of a parish community.

What is it like when you walk into your parish church on Sunday? Here is a check list for you to ponder:

- Do you feel that you've come home?
- Do you *know* people?
- Do they greet you?
- Do you feel welcomed?
- Is there an inviting feeling in the church? Is it clean and welcoming?
- Do the ministers invite you into worship?
- Does the priest ever invite you to greet your neighbor at the beginning of Mass?

- Is the liturgy gradually leading you into the arms of Jesus?
- Do you sense His presence? His embrace?
- Do you hold hands at the Lord's Prayer?
- Does the celebrant make it a time for uniting people of different colors, nationalities and religions into one people?
- Do you experience the love of the community praying for you and your needs?
- Is the sign of peace a beautiful and touching celebration of family?
- Does the celebrant greet you after Mass?
- Are the other clergy and staff there?
- Are you embraced?
- Are you welcomed if you are new?
- Do you feel like you're somebody special?
- Do you feel loved?
- Is there fellowship after Mass?
- Is the sacrament of friendship and love encouraged?
- Will you (as the title of this book suggests) go "from holy hour to happy hour"?

Love must be expressed and it must be celebrated. That's the job of the Church. Reviewing these questions about Sunday morning will help us to see if our parishes are truly moving to build communities where loved is expressed.

The Living Church

A great temptation is to run a parish like a business, making it a place that is very efficient and that does many good things. The problem is that our people don't need to be a part of another institution, good as it may be. They need to be part of a family.

The pastoral team that leads and serves a parish needs to examine their hearts and periodically evaluate whether the parish's priorities are correct. The healing miracles of Jesus give us the lead: people come first. They are more important than the arbitrary rules and regulations. Love has priority over efficiency and neatness. The "good" Church will always be in order and everyone will know his/her place. The "loving" Church will sometimes be a mess. Schedules and rules will stretch and sometimes even break. The "loving" Church will always be filled with laughter and joy. It will be crazy! How can we be that different from the God who loves us so insanely!

This love has to be experienced in all the aspects of parish life. People will not join or stay in the Church because of some great theological insight. They will be hugged into the Church and they will stay if they find God there. God is love. Jesus is the flesh and blood love of the Father. The Church continues to be his flesh and blood. Its main mission is to enable people to touch the loving God in the embrace of the community we call the Body of Christ.

Pastoral teams must create a variety of ways to tell God's people that they are loved and cherished, that they are important and welcomed, and that they must give away the gift that is given to them — love.

Chapter Five

Be Who You Are

So much of loving has to do with presence. Parish leadership has to be present to the people. Presence isn't just a pro forma "showing one's face." Presence means that I enjoy being here and that I'm glad that I'm with you. When Jesus ate out (which he did all the time) he didn't do it just because he was looking to make converts. He did it because he got a kick out of it. He enjoyed the people and the conversation. A lot of what Jesus talked about was not religious stuff. He seemed to love small talk and just "being." He enjoyed the food and drink. He enjoyed company.

The loving presence of the pastor and other parish ministers show how glad they are to be a part of the family. It says, "I'm pleased to be with you and I wonder what I'm going to learn from you today." Presence is not doing; it's not working the crowd; it's not achieving anything. It's just being who I am with you. I don't have to be Johnny Carson. I have to be me. Sometimes I'm boring, sometimes I'm entertaining and sometimes I'm brilliant. What really matters is that I just be me.

It goes without saying that the pastor and parish ministers must be present at moments like sickness or death. But presence is also imperative in the non-crisis moments — the relaxed and easy-going times when we just "hang out." If the pastor or parish minister are only present when they are "performing," then there is little chance of real relationship being formed. If I don't "waste time" with you, how can I ever have a relationship with you? Pastoral leadership has a lot to do with creating situations where God's people come together to do nothing more than be together. (In Part II of this book I will give some suggestions on how this can be done.)

The Sacramental Value of Presence

Today many of society's ills seem to stem from a lack of presence on the part of parents in the lives of children. The Church does a great service not only in calling people to be present, but also in teaching the sacramental value of presence. When we discover how beautiful we are, we begin to understand how important the gift of self truly is in the life of the Church and the family. There is no substitute for mommy and daddy just being there. Parents have to work hard today when finances demand so much of them in terms of jobs and hours out of the home. They have to carefully build into their lives quality time to "waste" with their children. I will speak of this later in terms of the Eucharist, but if families don't share at least a few real "Eucharistic" meals each week, they suffer for it.

So it is with parish family. Can we really celebrate the Eucharist if we don't experience "Eucharists" in the normal flow of parish life? How can I experience Jesus as I should at Mass if I don't experience Him in the presence and sacrament of sisters and brothers?

Interpersonal relationships sometimes get in the way of an efficient program. Jesus would never have made it in many of our parishes! His style seems to be completely anti-program and totally pro-people. Jesus *worked* at being with people. It didn't just happen. He sent out the message that he wanted to be disturbed and he wanted people to interrupt him. A lot of parishes give out the opposite message.

Sharing Responsibility and Work

In a false understanding of what the "new" Church is, leadership stresses the empowerment of the laity to the point of abdication of responsibility and presence on the part of leadership. True empowerment of the laity, however, demands the support and presence of leadership and the sharing of responsibility and work. It should never be an either/or proposition or an us/them situation. Rather, it's the whole Body working together and sharing the labor, pain and joy together.

It's great to have Eucharistic Ministers bring the Eucharist to the homebound and to visit the hospitalized. The pastoral leadership, hopefully, becomes very present to these ministers. They form them, encourage them and support them. It sometimes happens that, because lay people are doing pastoral tasks, the leadership stops doing them. Isn't it a strange paradox that there are parishes where the laity visit the sick and the clergy doesn't go near them except to give the last sacraments? Can that be good for the sick, not to mention the clergy?

Make no mistake about it, lay ministers do a much better job of pastoral visitation of the sick. The typical minister will spend a full hour with the sick person. They share prayer and conversation in a way that the clergy usually can't because of time and other factors. They establish a precious relationship with their homebound friend, which is an incredible gift to the homebound and to the minister as well. They become "specialists." Usually they become very significant people in the lives of the homebound, sometimes quasi-family members.

When the leadership of the parish abdicates direct "hands on" ministry, a structure is created where the clergy, religious and staff become remote persons who lose the human touch and the affirmation of direct person-to-person ministry. If lay members of the community are ministering to the sick, teaching, counseling, administrating and working with the youth, what is the leadership doing? Where are they? Who are they? Do they abdicate their pastoral duties and settle for being middle management bureaucrats who administer buildings and finances and run programs? These are necessary and good, and thank God, today many parishes have superb ministers of finance and administration who know what they are doing. Their ministry enables the parish to have the resources to be able to finance the ministries. These good people free the clergy and staff so that they can be involved in "hands on" people ministry.

We Are Family

For a parish to work, the leadership has to say in words and gestures: "We are here for you, we belong to you and you to us. We are family." A lot of parishes have become fortresses where the king and his court are inaccessible. It's dangerous to try to swim across the moat — some have alligators in them! The more situations that the leadership can create to be with the family, the more the message, "I love you" will be proclaimed. The more the leader is really known and perceived as a good and normal person, the more likely the people will be to bring him their problems.

Loving presence also teaches you how to live your daily life in such a way that you have the time and energy to be with your people in moments of death, crisis and celebration. Loving pastoral presence means that I'm walking with you and you're walking with me. As we do so, others follow the example and before you know it, a whole community is together and united in love, sharing the beautiful and painful moments of life together. Ministry is done by everybody — including the professionals!

Chapter Six

The Endurance of Loving Commitment

Loving means commitment. When we prepare couples for marriage, commitment is a big issue. For a love to endure it must be the pledge of my life to you forever, "in good times and in bad." I don't stay with you because things are going well or because I'm successful. I stay with you because I belong to you and you belong to me. There's no getting out; there are no loopholes.

In reality, sticking together when it's tough strengthens the bond, and it endures forever. My parents never reminisced about their successes, only about the days when they had nothing but each other. They took delight in telling the story of looking all over for pennies so that they could buy a bottle of beer to celebrate an anniversary. It's the sticking together in tough times that empowers a relationship to make it through anything — even success! The same holds true of parish life.

There are wonderful times and there are terrible times. When we stick together in the terrible days, the other days are even more glorious because we've been through it together. When the people have a sense that the priest is there to stay, they will be there to stay. When the parish is a "stepping stone" to bigger and better things, the people know it. They are never able to give it everything because their leader is neither willing, nor able, to do so.

A parish will never develop to its fullest potential if there is a basic lack of understanding of being a family in which commitments are made and kept. I cannot be your sister or brother one day and a stranger the next. Family demands permanency, or else it becomes sick. There are too many parish communities where growth can't take place because the shepherds are hired hands. Their work is rooted in power or prestige or security, not love. Because they do not see their role as laying down their lives for the flock, the flock is always divided and never really one.

Seeking the Lord Together

We delude ourselves into believing that "good" liturgies, great programs and more adult education will make our parishes great. Nothing can ever make them great except becoming devoted and loving families. These families are composed of sisters and brothers committed to seeking the Lord together. That commitment starts with the leadership and they model this way of life to all the community. The parish family living in covenant becomes a model to each of the families of the parish.

When we "get it" about commitment, parish outreach to the poor inevitably follows. People become very giving and generous when they realize that they truly are sisters and brothers and that they have a responsibility to one another because they are family. Indeed, every ministry in the parish flowers when we realize that every family impacts on the larger parish family. Parish thrives because you belong to me and I belong to you. As I come to believe that I am part of the Body of Christ, my dedication to the Lord Jesus grows as my commitment to my neighbor grows.

The Eucharist Reinforces Our Commitment

We affirm our pledge to "stick together" every Sunday as we celebrate the Eucharist. The celebration itself is an experience and reinforcement of Christian community. When Eucharist is celebrated in a real community, it's not possible to remain in a "Jesus and me" spirituality. The need for and the commitment to the family is experienced powerfully at every Eucharist.

Obviously, this is not "fulfilling an obligation" spirituality. In the committed community, people come to Mass because they need Jesus in the Eucharist and because they need one another, which is really the same thing. In the committed parish family, people don't know what you mean by "obligation attendance" at Mass. They are there because they can't live without Jesus and without each other.

The celebration of the Eucharist is the means by which the parish is re-created and re-committed each week. The process is ongoing and never ceases, because we never completely become what Jesus is calling us to be. Our commitment demands that we never stop, because we are not only committed to Jesus and to each other, we are committed to growth and transformation which never comes to an end.

The loving commitment to the parish is to a deepening of love with Jesus and to one another. It is a commitment to love and holiness. It is a commitment to life and growth. It is a commitment to new life and excellence. It never ends. It cannot, because we can never possess all of God.

Chapter Seven

The Cost of Community

The price of community is real, and it is costly. It is the laying down of one's life for the parish family. Every leadership person and eventually each member of the community must be ready and willing to pay this price if there is going to be a real family.

But the laying down of one's life is *not* committing suicide. It is not killing oneself or burning oneself out. It is not working oneself to death. The laying down of one's life is the *gift* of oneself to the community, but this gift of self is characterized by common sense and balance.

Effective Ministry Is a Sensible Investment

People who are in ministry sometimes go to the excesses of escapism or annihilation. There is a prudent, sensible, middle way that we all have to try to achieve. We can only do what we *can* do. If we drive ourselves to the point of exhaustion and irritability, do we really help anyone? What good is it if we are never *really* present to people in their needs because of our own fatigue and distraction? What good is it to work all day long and find no satisfaction in what we are doing? Work that should give life becomes drudgery and a burden.

Many ministers are afraid to get close to their people and never do so, because they are afraid of being eaten alive. The signal goes out that he or she "runs" programs and administers buildings, but doesn't get close to anyone. People like this do what they are required to do, but no more. They are efficient, punctual and dependable. They are also aloof, removed and never emotionally involved in what they are doing.

Others take the world upon themselves and never say "no." They never think of their own needs. For them zeal and devotion mean a total commitment of self with no time for themselves or their families or for their own growth and development, not to mention needs. While one may admire their dedication, the tragic result of a lifestyle that's always giving and always involved will result in sickness, loss of faith, disillusionment and possibly leaving the ministry, disgruntled and unfulfilled. It can even lead to the break up of the family for lay ministers.

There has to be another way and there is. *I can only do what I can do*. That changes at different times of my life. In prayer I have to beg Jesus to guide me with his Holy Spirit so that I can know "how much" and "what" is expected of me. I have to ask the Lord honestly to let me know when I'm being lazy and selfish. I have to allow the Spirit to correct me of my pride and egoism when I'm doing too much. I also have to let the Spirit and my family and friends console me when I'm overdoing it and I need to be consoled.

The Tools of the Trade

Prayer is the answer. Loving conversation with Jesus will tell me everything I have to know about my ministry and my lifestyle. Spiritual directors and family and friends will also guide me. I need friends who will challenge me as well as console and reassure me.

The life of the Lord will be the guide for the minister. Jesus did not cure everyone who was ill. He did not console everyone who was troubled. He did not make every party. He did not fulfill everybody's expectation of him. He couldn't physically or emotionally be everything to everyone who needed him. He needed to be alone to pray. He needed to relax with good friends like Martha, Mary and Lazarus who were not always talking about religion. He needed to go to His mother's house to sleep and have a good meal.

Jesus gave Himself completely, but He still was able to have a life outside of ministry. His life outside of ministry refreshed him and let him return "raring to go." Are we any different than Jesus? We all have the need for the things that make a person human — intimacy, affection, prayer, friendship, family, art, music, reading and exercise. How can we fully minister if we're not fully human?

The minister will not be afraid if he or she trusts in the Lord's care and the Lord's providence. He or she will create the atmosphere where the Lord's work will be done and he or she will do loads of it, but *never* all of it. It is always unfinished. The gift of the minister is to create the atmosphere where there is enough love and faith present for everyone to believe in their own giftedness and their responsibility to use their gifts for the building up of the Body of Christ. That's how the work gets done. *Nobody* does it all alone!

The Lord Knows Best

Each of us will learn what He wants of us when we ask Him. It's as simple as that. It's His Church and He will take very good care of it. He will use you to do His work and He expects the total gift of your heart and your life. He wants you to work hard and to be very generous. He wants you to give your life for your flock, but He does not want you to commit suicide in the process. He wants to get *lots* of years and *lots* of work out of you. Trust Him. He knows best!

Each of us must learn that we do not build the Kingdom by the amount of work we do, but by the intensity of our love for the Lord and our people. It is only that deep and sincere love that calls people to life. It is that love that creates a revolution in a community and it is that love that causes real change and transformation. The Lord will teach us how to love, but only *we* make the decision to love. It is that decision, like that of Mary at the Annunciation, that can change and bring new life and recreate the face of the earth: "All generations shall call me blessed for He who his mighty has done great things for me and holy is His name" (Luke 1:48). This beautiful prayer of praise of Mary is our prayer when we allow the Lord to run His Church as we do His holy will.

New Life Is Possible for Everyone

Some who read this will be in parishes where the community and family we yearn for has not yet come to be. They may not be in leadership roles and may feel powerless to bring about change. They are not! Many parishes begin to be transformed when a few of the saints begin to gather in prayer in His name. It is their prayer and fasting that brings the graces of the Holy Spirit, which cause new life and new beginnings.

If we really believe that Jesus is present when two or three gather in His name, then we have to believe that the gathering in His name is Creation. It is Genesis. It is the beginning. Once it begins, no matter how simply or humbly, community and family will come to be. Moses did not live to see the promised land, yet Israel reached it. You may not live to see the promised land either, but remember: What the Lord asks of us is not success but fidelity.

When we are able to love the Lord and His people so powerfully, then it doesn't matter if we succeed or not; the victory in Christ Jesus is guaranteed. So many have never lived to see the Promised Land, yet their being faithful was the reaching of the Promised Land. Their fidelity was the fulfillment of the Promise. Their unwavering "yes," like Mary's, began the new world. When Jesus was alive within her, God was with us. When we say our "yes" even when it seems useless and hopeless, the Word has become flesh. He is with us. It is only a matter of time before He will be born for all to see.

In the great successful parish families, in the struggling places trying so hard to become communities, in the places where there seems to be no hope of a family ever being born, all it takes is for you and me to say our "yes." When we do so, the Incarnation begins again and Christ is alive among His people. The seemingly insignificant mustard seed will grow into the magnificent tree of life for all people. Our puny, weak, and struggling "yes" will make all the difference. It's all that the Lord needs to do His mighty work. Are we willing to pay the price?

Part Two
Practical Ways to Celebrate Community

Chapter Eight

Creating Community

In the first part of this book we have looked at what is the essential ingredient of a parish. It is love. It is relationship. It is experiencing the presence of Christ in the community. It is knowing I belong and that I am an essential part of the family. It is communication. It is prayer of the heart. It is feeling and knowing that I am a part of a living Body rather than a member of an organization called Church.

We have also seen that these community/family aspects of Church and parish come to be as the leadership and eventually all the members become converted and are willing to pay the price for community by laying down their lives in love for one another.

This part of the book will try to give some very practical suggestions on how to go about achieving and creating this Family/Church atmosphere which we all so much desire. These suggestions are tried and true attempts to create community. But they are not gimmicks without substance. If they don't flow from the loving and concerned hearts of the leadership they will fail and actually be counterproductive. *Nothing works if the parish is not seen and experienced as family.*

The Filling Station

One of the models of parish that has been decried as weak and incomplete is that of the filling station. In this model the parish dispenses the sacraments necessary for salvation but offers little more for the spiritual life of the people. Actually, the filling station model has value *if* we see the home Church as the real Church and the parish's role as one of affirming and strengthening what happens in the sacrament of family.

This model sees holiness not as the gift given to the Christian by the Church, but rather sees the Christian as *already* possessing holiness through living the sacraments of baptism, marriage and parenthood. When the community comes together to celebrate the Eucharist, the Church doesn't make God's people holy, but rather reminds them of what they already possess. In this view the Church doesn't sanctify the people; the people sanctify the Church.

It is the job of the Church leaders at Sunday Mass to open the eyes of the people and to remind them of who they are and what they are called to become because of who they are. The Sunday Eucharist is meant to provide nourishment, strength, forgiveness, reconciliation and encouragement so that we may go home and live the Christian life and create Church at home and at work. The real experience of Church and Christ will not come in a church building but in the faithful living out of the relationships in one's life. Our holiness is in *being* wife, mother, husband, parent, friend, nun, priest, etc., to the best of our ability. Like Jesus, we are called to lay down our lives in the gift of love.

The Monastery

So much of Catholic spirituality is still understood in the mentality of flight from the "world." I become holy as I get away from my husband, wife or parishioners (for the priest). The true place to find God is in the quiet of retreats and visits to the Blessed Sacrament. These are considered the true moments of holiness because I am alone with God and free of all the distractions of my life, like my kids and spouse.

Imagine what this mentality does to Catholic couples! Many *good* husbands and wives are troubled about their sexual relationship because they've never been told that the greatest moment of intimacy with the passionate God is sexual intimacy. A couple experiences the powerful love of God as they discover and celebrate each other in flesh and mind and spirit.

If we give the illusion that the Church and its sacraments are holier than the vocation and sacramental lives of the people, we distort the very meaning of the holiness of the lives of the baptized.

What Is the Church For?

The Church does an indispensable job in gathering its people each week to remind them of who they are and what they already possess. The Church encourages the people to *live* the life to which they have been called. We remind one another of what Jesus has given us and what Jesus calls us to be.

We are challenged to truly see and understand what we already possess. Just because one has a child doesn't mean that one is a real parent. The Church has an incredible challenge — to help its people live the mystery and the gift that God has given to them.

The Church reminds husbands and wives that as they touch and love each other they do so to Christ. The Church reminds the couple that the living out of their marriage covenant is the most authentic and life-giving experience of Jesus that they will ever know. Really, being husband, wife, parent, friend, sister or brother *is* holiness. The Church has nothing to give us but the constant reminder of the power and the holiness that we already possess.

To be faithful to what we are is to be constantly entering into the Paschal Mystery of Jesus — His Death and Resurrection. I can never be the priest, friend, sister, brother, spouse or parent that my holiness calls me to unless I am dying to the selfishness, smallness and pettiness that prevents me from giving the gift of my life to my beloved.

A Tough Gospel

To call people to this fidelity and to their identity is to call them to a very strict and demanding Gospel. It is to demand nothing less than the imitation of Christ and His total love of His beloved Spouse — the Church. This reminder will cause a revolution in family life as couples and families achieve a new confidence in their worth and value. They will realize that their home is not a stepchild of the Church but is *really* the Church. The domestic Church is the primary experience of God's love and mercy in our life. Our people are called to be the Church — the Body of Christ in this world — beginning at home.

A Social Gospel

The more we claim our identity, the more we become aware of and faithful to our relationships. Our first experience of Jesus should always be in our homes. From there we will celebrate the presence of the Lord in the parish community. When we celebrate the Eucharist together and realize that we must *be* Eucharist to one another, then we will want to experience and touch Jesus in the poor of the community and the world.

In parishes where community is formed in homes and in larger church gatherings, a compassion for and reaching out to the poor always follows. As I begin to realize who I am and who you are, I then begin to understand who the poor are — my sisters and brothers in Christ.

It is obvious from the brokenness of today's society that the power of the holiness of family life is not being realized. Family life is hurting. Divorce, separation, couples living together before marriage, abortion, pornography — all these things hurt families. Parents work longer and harder than they did a generation ago and have less leisure time. All of this points out how much work the parish has to do to minister to families.

We see much more emphasis on marriage and baptism preparation as well as Family Life programs and family-centered CCD and school programs in the Church today. But that is not enough. In addition to the liturgy on Sunday nourishing the holiness of all relationships, the Church has to make it clear by *all* its activities that the family is its paramount concern and hope. All parishes need more opportunities for families to preach and to share their experience of God and what they are looking for from the Church as well as for the parish to listen to their needs and hopes. It must also provide opportunities for the people to tell their faith stories.

The Cloister Has a Place

Far from minimizing the times and places of quiet meditation, we see how essential the cloister and opportunities for prayer are. They are needed to re-focus our lives and to see and touch the holy and the presence of God in our daily lives and our relationships. All the wonderful experiences of prayer that the Catholic tradition has to offer including Sunday Mass have one common purpose: to enable me to return to my real life and truly see and understand it for what it is — the Kingdom of God.

In the pages that follow I will take you into the life of St. Brigid's Parish to see what has worked for us to enhance and create community and family. The common thrust is this: to enable people to recognize and to live the holiness of their daily lives.

Chapter Nine

We Celebrate Birth

The birth of a child is perhaps the greatest opportunity for a parish to touch, teach and inspire a couple as they begin a new phase of their life together. A parish has to give its best to make the birth and baptism of each child a profoundly moving and religious experience of life and hope.

Mass for Expectant Parents

Twice a year at a Sunday Mass we invite all of our expectant parents to be prayed over and blessed as we pray for a safe and healthy delivery. I'll make a point now that will be repeated many times: *there are blessings and there are blessings!* It is absolutely imperative that the priest and members of the team *touch and embrace* the couples.

I begin by inviting the couples into the sanctuary at the Lord's Prayer. When they are gathered around the altar, I ask the congregation to raise their hands in prayer over the couples. Then the baptism team couples and I go from couple to couple laying on hands and communicating to each of these couples the love and holiness of God's people and our joy and happiness that they are going to have a baby. I conclude by asking the congregation to join hands and pray the Lord's Prayer together.

What a Sign of Peace follows! The parish family has shown its love for these couples and made their joy its joy. What a celebration of life and love — with Jesus present on the altar in the Eucharist these couples are reminded that they must be Eucharist to each other and to their baby! There are few moments filled with such love and joy. When we embrace and love our expectant couples — that's being a Pro-Life Parish!

As I said earlier, there are blessings and there are blessings. Some parishes have their hearts in the right place and want to celebrate life. They will have Masses for expectant parents during which they may ask the couples to rise in place and say some little prayer for them, or they may make a limp reference to them in the Prayer of the Faithful (similar to what's suggested on Mother's Day or Father's Day). Mass is really celebrated *for* expectant parents when *they* become the main focus of the liturgy, sermon, prayers and special activities. They need to be touched, anointed, held and loved by the community. And Sunday Mass is the place to do it. The blessings that flow to all present are very obvious and powerful.

Such a liturgy has to be very emotional. It must touch the hearts of the couples and everyone else who is in the church. The skilled celebrant knows how to include the appropriate readings, adapt the prayers and call for the love and the affirmation of the community for these couples. When they experience a real blessing from a loving family they will never forget it.

It goes without saying that there should be fellowship after the Mass to continue the celebration. Fellowship provides the atmosphere for the cultivation of Christian friendship — the greatest of all sacraments. When this kind of community is alive in the parish, pastors hear parishioners say they would never want to leave the area because of the parish. That's music to our ears!

I know this sounds extreme, but I believe as much can happen during fellowship after Mass as during Mass itself. If we really understand what Eucharist is, then it makes great sense to believe that the power of Christ's love touches us as deeply when we gather in His name in love as when we receive Holy Communion.

The Rite of Baptism

The new Rite of Baptism encourages the Church to prepare the parents and God-parents for a meaningful celebration of the sacrament. Unfortunately, many Baptism Preparation sessions become a time for lecturing and rule-giving rather than for exploring the religious dimensions of the most religious of all experiences: bringing a child into the world. The preparation and session should really be an evening of prayer for the parents.

I suggest that every session to which you invite adults be extremely well organized, that the team be well prepared and that the goals and objectives of the classes be clear. Don't waste time on the superficial or "rules" unless you're questioned. Such items can be thoroughly covered in hand-outs. Make the session an opportunity for the couples to reflect upon and speak about the spiritual reality of the birth of *their* child. What is God doing in *their* lives?

Our Baptism Prep Evening of Prayer takes place in church. For many of the couples that in itself is a homecoming. We try to welcome them and remind them that the Church is *their* home and that they are always welcome to "drop in" and speak to the Lord.

At St. Brigid's two married couples and a priest or deacon make the presentations. The session begins with the Liguori video tape, *Your Child's Baptism* (the best I have ever seen). It is a very healing and consoling story of a few families celebrating baptism. The theology is good and the overall effect is relaxing and welcoming.

One of the team couples then welcomes everyone and asks them all to introduce themselves and then opens with a prayer. Each parent is given a booklet in which they individually write their responses to questions about faith and baptism. After they have finished, they are asked to share their answers with their spouse, not with the group. The questions ask the couple to talk about their reasons for baptizing their child, their goals for their religious life, their faith life together, etc. They take this exercise very seriously and take the booklet home for future discussion.

Next, the married couple team members speak about *their* faith and the baptism of their own children. The stories are very personal and very real. They help the participants to see that active Catholics are real and believable people and that *they* can be a part of the Church, too.

After the couples speak, the priest or deacon gives a welcoming talk. He stresses the holiness of bringing a child into the world, the sacredness of their life together, and the precious gift their love for each other is. He encourages the new parents to allow the Church to help them as they connect with other people like themselves who are trying to raise their children with values. The talk should include the experience of adoptive parents as well.

At this point, each participant is given, in a very nonthreatening way, an opportunity to share something. The session ends with a prayer for families. The participants are given materials, one of which is *Your Child's Baptism* by Liguori Publications. People do read pertinent and well-written materials.

The Outline of the Session

Participants gather in main body of church.

8:00 P.M. Video by Liguori Publications:
Your Child's Baptism

8:20 P.M. Welcome — Team Couple
Introductions
Prayer

8:25 P.M. Workbooks are given out.
(*Soft music in background*)
Couples answer questions privately and then share their answers with each other.

9:05 P.M. Couples are called together in a circle
(*in the Blessed Sacrament Chapel*)
Couples give talk
Priest gives talk

9:25 P.M. Each participant is asked to share:
"How did I feel when I looked at my newborn baby?"
"What do I want for my newborn baby?"

9:45 P.M. Closing Prayer: Team Couple
The couples are invited to inscribe their children's name in the "Book of Remembrance" near the tabernacle. They love that!

Our feedback from the parents has been very positive. Many linger for conversation after the session ends. The heart of the sessions is the sharing of the team couples and the sharing of the participants. They are led to share the spiritual dimensions of what they have just experienced at the birth of their child. Hopefully, it will make the baptism much more meaningful.

The Baptism Ceremony

The key to making baptisms special is the presence of a hostess who assists the priest or deacon with the ceremony. She places a name plate on the pew reserved for each family and will usually act as lector and assistant during the ceremony. Before the ceremony, the hostess welcomes and seats the family. The sacred nature of what is happening is enhanced with recorded music. Our hostesses have made baptism ceremonies much more welcoming and have greatly added to the dignity and sacredness of the ceremony.

After the Baptism

It is a wonderful gesture to send a card to the babies on the anniversary of their baptism, but sometimes couples with toddlers can be a neglected part of the parish.

In fact many couples comment that the Church did a good job in preparing them for marriage with Pre-Cana, but no one prepared them for the adjustment needed at the birth of a child. The more enrichment experiences that the parish can offer to new parents as their lives change physically, psychologically and sexually, the greater will be the benefit for these couples as well as for the whole parish. We find that our literature and courses in parenting are gratefully received by the couples. When the Church loves and serves family it becomes the Church of the People that is more believable because it understands and because it really tries to reach out and help.

Reunion of the Babies

On the Feast of the Baptism of Christ we invite all the babies who were baptized during the year to a special liturgy. A humorous letter tells the children not to be embarrassed by their parents if they squirm or make noise because parents are like that! The message assures the parents that the parish is "children friendly" and that their children belong there.

During this Mass, the prayers, sermon and activities are directed to the families and their children. Imagine your church filled with over one hundred children less than a year old with their families! The family is together. There is life and joy.

Similar to the Mass for Expectant Parents, the parents and children are brought up to the altar at the time of the Lord's Prayer for a special blessing. All join hands for the Lord's Prayer and exchange a most joyful Sign of Peace. Christ's life fills the church in the exuberance and vitality of these young members of the Body of Christ.

After Mass on this day we have fellowship but with a

few flourishes. On the church lawn we have a life-size Nativity scene. On this day we enhance it with live animals. The babies are invited to "stand in" for Baby Jesus in the manger. Baby after baby is placed in the manger by Shepherdess Mary Schlaich to the clicking of cameras and the delight of parents, grandparents and all present. Hot chocolate and refreshments are served as Diego takes the older children for a ride in the pony cart.

The day always proves to be a glorious celebration of family and parish. The message the parish is giving is obvious. I cannot tell you how positive the response of parents and visitors is to this Mass. People love a parish that loves their children and grandchildren. A parish that cherishes and loves its young people creates an atmosphere where there is warmth, affection and trust. People never forget what you do for their children. Jesus with the children in His arms is our model.

Mothers' Support Groups

We have seen the growth of Mothers' Prayer Groups in the parish as more young mothers look for and appreciate meeting with their peers for mutual support and prayer. The spiritual life of their families is deepened as they come together to share their lives and their struggles. Young children are introduced to the reality that prayer is not just for church, as they see their moms pray with their friends. The base community becomes the Church for these mothers and their family.

Mass for Infertile Couples – St. Gerard Majella

St. Gerard is the patron of mothers. He is also the patron saint of couples who have difficulty in conceiving. This year we introduced a Mass on his feast day, October 15, for those couples. We pray over them and we anoint them and bless them with the relic of St. Gerard. What we do is to give the Church and Jesus the opportunity to hold in its arms these couples who so yearn for a child. I stress: *hold* them in *our* arms! Another opportunity is created for the Church to show its love and care. Many of the couples aren't churchgoers, but they are touched and they look at the Church in a whole new way — especially if they get pregnant — and some always do. It's amazing what the Holy Spirit is able to accomplish through our feeble efforts. A follow-up Mass card and/or phone call makes the experience even more effective. The Church (Jesus) continues to reach out and say, I love you.

Ministry to All Families

Religious Ed, School and Family Life Ministries are great ways for a parish to keep before itself the goal of affirming and serving families — all kinds of families. The single parent family must feel as important as any other. Parishioners need to see such families involved in and participating in all parish activities. A very special affirmation of a family is to call them forth by name to dress the altar or bring up the gifts at Sunday liturgy. The more we single out and honor families the more we affirm them and say how important they are in the life of a parish.

The "norm" of parish life is family. Family isn't just tolerated, it is the main ingredient of parish life. Our model of Church often is the monastery or the middle-aged or elderly Catholic. Since I am in the latter group I'm the first to say that they also have needs that should be ministered to. (They are the ones who are the greatest financial supporters of the Church. God bless them!) But the Church has no future if families aren't given the place of prominence they deserve. Family life ministry isn't patronizing. It is realistic. It is guaranteeing that there *will* be a Church in the next generation. Besides all that, it's so much fun!

Chapter Ten

We Celebrate Marriage

Marriage preparation is very problematic at this time in the Church's life. We are all committed to the meaning of the sacrament, but divorce rates indicate that somehow we're not getting the job done. We question whether our Pre-Cana approach has value for couples living together before marriage. The number of people who come from divorced or dysfunctional families causes us to re-evaluate everything we are doing in marriage preparation. We are living in a new world and the Church has to invest more of its resources to serve and help our young people.

All of this being true, there is no moment in Church life with greater opportunities for evangelization and outreach than marriage preparation.

Pre-Cana

There are many resources available to help structure an In-Home Pre-Cana program. The parish has the perfect ingredients for a successful and dynamic program. It has happily married and holy married couples who can be mentors and companions to engaged couples on their journey to the altar.

A parish Pre-Cana Program has to be planned by the married couples and the clergy together. The "course" is meant to surface issues and areas of concern that are present in every marriage through the real life sharing of the team couples. They do not teach. They speak of real issues and problems. They share their values and their faith in Jesus. They are role models of what Christian marriage is all about.

The engaged couples need materials to read and discuss, not only for their own personal growth, but to bring life and excitement to the home sessions. The leaders have to draw the couples out so that they will share their own journey with the group.

Pre-Cana can and does make a tremendous difference in the marriages of the couples who participate. The young couples must be welcomed for who they are. They must not be judged but rather made to feel a part of a family that perhaps they haven't known for a while. Many couples return to Church when the priest or deacon who does the preliminary paper work gently *invites* them to come home. When the couple senses that the Church is really interested in them, not for the wedding fee or anything else but *themselves,* they warm up and at least begin to listen.

For many couples the Pre-Cana team couple will be the only people with whom they can really talk about their concerns. Many can't or won't talk seriously about the marriage with their parents or friends. What a blessing to a young couple to have people like this who are there for them during their engagement and later in their marriage. There is a great likelihood that a couple who experiences the ministry of the Body of Christ in such a way will themselves become active in ministry as their marriage and life develop.

We try to share with our engaged couples everything we believe about Christ-centered family life. They must hear about the holiness of marriage. They must know that God is giving them everything in giving them each other. They must understand that their love for each other is the holiest thing in their life and that as they love each other they love God. They must know that their sexual love is an experience of the passionate God who is present to them in the passion and power of their love.

What a challenge Pre-Cana presents to a parish. We can do it! We have the greatest ingredient — happy and holy couples who are willing to share their life and their sacrament with young couples who are holy enough and crazy enough to want to get married.

We offer our Pre-Cana Program at St. Brigid's three times a year. Let's look at how we structure it.

1. The couple calls the Church office for an appointment to set the date of their marriage. They are mailed a booklet containing pertinent information about marriage in the parish.

2. The couple has an initial meeting with a priest or deacon. They fill out the necessary papers and talk about their relationship and their sacrament.

3. Pre-Cana begins at 1:00 P.M. Mass on Sunday. The engaged couples are prayed for and blessed at the Mass. An organizational meeting follows to set up Home Meetings. The pastor assumes the role of Papa and speaks to the couples about their parish Pre-Cana and the sacrament of marriage and tries to set the tone of how important Pre-Cana is to the parish.

4. The next four sessions take place in the homes of the team couples. There are five or six engaged couples in a group. Topics like communication, sexuality, children, finances, and spirituality are discussed.

5. An evening of prayer is conducted by the parish priests for the couples. Confession is available. The evening ends with Mass and the blessing of the engagement rings.

6. A week later a closing Pre-Cana Mass and fellowship bring the Pre-Cana session to a close. The parents and the wedding parties of the couples are also invited.

7. The couples meet to discuss music selections with the parish musicians prior to the ceremony.

8. The celebrant — priest or deacon — of the ceremony meets with the couples to discuss the Pre-Cana experience and go over the wedding liturgy.

The Ceremony

The wedding liturgy is a very important moment of evangelization for the couple, their families and the many guests. Some of them haven't been to church in years. The priest or deacon and music ministers have the possibility of moving hearts and leading people gently home to Jesus. When the Church comes off as the defender of love and commitment and as the proclaimer of the Gospel of people's holiness, an opportunity is created for people to take a second look at the Church and their relationship to it. The Pre-Cana team couples also attend their couple's wedding as a sign of their love and support, and the parish's as well.

Marriage is a golden opportunity for the Church to passionately and proudly love this couple as they make their vows. It also becomes the opportunity to empower and send forth the couple as missionaries of God's love. Their home — the domestic Church — becomes the place where God dwells because of the love they share with each other and eventually with their children. The Sunday Eucharist is meant to be the weekly celebration and renewal of the covenant of their love in Christ Jesus our Lord.

So many times priests don't look forward to weddings because they often have to deal with the "unchurched" and the ceremony becomes uncomfortable for them. Perhaps that is because we have forgotten the missionary impetus of Christ's Church — to reach out to the stray sheep.

The parish has several months to work with a couple. We have the chance to evangelize, personally welcome home, teach and celebrate the sacraments. Not everyone will accept our invitation. Not everyone accepted Jesus' invitation. But some will. More than we suspect. There are so many who are just waiting for the invitation to come home to the

Lord. An invitation is really the experience of being loved and welcomed. (Our Pre-Cana team couples are experts at that.) Don't write any couple off. Do for them what Jesus would do. Give them a chance to find their faith.

It is important to make a big deal in the parish bulletin about who is getting married. Announce their wedding day and ask for the prayers of the community for the couples being married. Give your best to the celebration. Help them plan the liturgy. Really celebrate the liturgy. It is the greatest day of their lives. Celebrate with excitement and joy. Pray and preach from the heart. Make it clear to everyone that Jesus is taking their hands in His in joining them as husband and wife.

Lay hands on the couple as you pray the Nuptial Blessing. Expand on the Blessing to include their history, their dreams and God's challenge to the couple. It's a beautiful gesture to have the couple's parents also lay hands on them as the Nuptial blessing is prayed. At the Lord's Prayer have the whole church join hands, even across the aisles, as a sign of what this couple is already doing for the Church — bringing unity and peace. Be sure to mention close relatives who have died in the prayer of the faithful.

At the time of Communion remind the couple and everyone else that they are now renewing the vows they made a few moments ago. That is what the Eucharist is — the renewal of our covenant of love in the Body and Blood of the Lord Jesus Christ. Imagine what would be happening in our parishes if each Eucharist were truly the renewal of our love and commitment to the Lord and to one another!

After the Ceremony

It is important for the young married couples to know that the clergy and couples who were there for them before the wedding will be there for them after their marriage. They only have to call them.

Parishes are becoming more aware that there is a need for

marriage enrichment programs and counseling in the parish setting. We often act as if "they lived happily ever after" was the reality of married life. For many it is not. The parish has to be there to encourage and to challenge couples to work hard on their marriages all through their married life.

So many marriages could be saved if couples had alternatives such as: peer counseling, support groups, therapy and spiritual direction. A *real* Pre-Cana can help a couple to discover if they "have the stuff to make it work." What has happened in our society is that the first marriage is the trial marriage or the *real* Pre-Cana. After the pain of divorce with its sobering and painful effects on the couple (and the children) a more serious and realistic man or woman can choose a more compatible mate.

It seems incredible that a Church that teaches the indissolubility of marriage can be so lackadaisical about whom they will marry and so careless in helping the couples after they wed. The time to discover that a couple is incompatible is *before* the marriage, not after. Isn't it better to use our resources as a Church to build good and healthy marriages rather than to annul them? Marriage Preparation and Family Ministry has to be the first priority of a parish. If it is not, we will wake up some day and discover that we have no parishes.

St. Valentine's Day

Because all that we have said about marriage applies to St. Valentine's Day, I turn to it now. The Church needs to celebrate human sexual love. It needs the input, teaching and preaching of happily married couples who are willing and able to celebrate the mystery and the sacrament of their sexual love. The way for most Christians to God is through sexual love and intimacy. This love is not something just tolerated to control "concupiscence." This love is an experience of the passion of the living God.

The Church is only beginning to put together a true theology of sex and marriage. It will take a long time for the Church to use images of God and prayer to express our body, sexual intimacy and pleasure. Our image of God is still basically, "the distant one," and the one we reach through self abnegation and penance. What a shock it is for married couples to learn that their love and intimacy is the closest that one can ever be to God in this life!

Our parishes are too "celibate" in their spirituality and religious expression. A new language and liturgy has to be created that is truly incarnational and that recognizes the sexual God who woos us and calls us into unity and love.

Our parishes have to celebrate love and commitment. A yearly celebration of love on St. Valentine's Day and World Marriage Day is a good beginning. They are opportunities for married couples to lead and to preach. What a blessing comes to the parish when it celebrates the love of its people.

World Marriage Sunday

Each year we celebrate a special Mass on World Marriage Sunday to honor our married couples celebrating their twenty-fifth and fiftieth wedding anniversaries. The church is packed and the spirit is contagious. How absolutely perfect it is for the Church to say "thank you" for all these years of loving fidelity. What a blessing these couples are to the parish and to the world.

After the Mass the parish hosts a reception for all these beautiful people. Each couple is presented with a marriage cross and scroll honoring them. How important it is for the Church to express its pride and gratitude to its beloved people for their great achievement.

Celebrate Love

Married love is not the only kind of love. Friendship and single parenthood are very special forms of love. There are many ways of loving. It's impossible to categorize them all, let alone place judgment on them. The Church has to love all people. Our arms have to be open to everyone. When we make it known that everyone is loved and no one is turned away, we begin to experience a special kind of Church.

Homosexuals have to be welcomed like everyone else. Our job is to embrace and love all of God's people; we must welcome them and leave the judgment to the Lord.

This is difficult terrain, but one thing is certain: the Church's arms must be open in love to welcome everyone and to remind them that the only thing that matters is love. At the heart of this love, the Church that teaches Christ's Word must be humble enough to trust their people as they discern their way with the guidance of the Holy Spirit. Sometimes what people discover through prayer and dialogue does not reach some of the ideals taught by the Church. The decisions we make based on our conscience must be accepted and respected even when the Church teaches and believes another ideal.

Chapter Eleven

We Bury Our Dead

The time of death is one of the most sensitive in the life of a parish. A parish that is able to identify with the pain of a family and walk with them truly ministers in the name of Jesus. While we preach a Gospel of Resurrection and life, we should not fail to react to death the way Jesus did at the death of Lazarus. The scene of Jesus arriving at Bethany is a perfect lesson for the minister to the bereaved. Notice what Jesus does *not* do: He does not speak pious platitudes; He does not tell them Lazarus is in a better place. No. Jesus does the most human thing possible: He weeps.

When someone in our parish dies, we are not called upon primarily to teach or to preach to the family. We are called upon to *be* with them and *share* their pain and grief. A trained minister can do all the professional things — only a brother and sister in Christ is able to share the pain and the hurt of a family mourning for a beloved husband, wife, child, parent or friend.

The parish is able to make a tremendous impact on a family at the time of death. It is a special time in which people are looking for a gentle and loving welcome home. It is a time to heal past hurts and wounds. It is a time for the clergy and staff to become acquainted with families who have fallen through the cracks over the years.

The Funeral Parlor

The wake service and the visitation time are moments for the clergy to get to know about the deceased by allowing the family and friends to share memories of the deceased. This can be a beautiful part of the wake service. It is a great preparation for the homily at the funeral Mass.

Obviously, it's the time to get to know the survivors themselves. It's a tender healing time. Families are so appreciative when clergy or staff members pay their respects. This simple gesture of family and friendship speaks volumes as to what the parish is all about.

The Funeral Mass

The same kinds of people are present at a funeral as are present at a wedding. There are always people ready and waiting to hear the word of welcome and to hear again about God who loves us passionately and constantly invites us to accept His love and friendship.

The celebration should flow from the kind of person we're burying. In rare cases when the person is not considered to be a sterling character, then we have to stress the mercy of God. But when the deceased is obviously a very good person, the celebration should be more of a canonization. Some funerals are nothing short of the public acclamation of the sanctity of an individual. They can have all the certainty and joy of a canonization in St. Peter's in Rome. The people declare by acclamation that the deceased is a saint of God. What can we add to that other than: Amen!

The family and friends should be encouraged to choose and proclaim the readings as well as bring the gifts to the altar and participate in the celebration. A eulogy presented by a family member or friend after Communion puts a personal touch to the end of the Mass. It helps to give the speaker suggestions about the length and delivery. Usually, they should be written out ahead of time and read.

At the cemetery we all come face to face with our mortality: dust to dust; ashes to ashes. Don't try to deny it or camouflage it. Accept it, but also declare once again our faith in the Lord's resurrection and in our loved one's resurrection.

After the Funeral

It's very important to keep in touch with the family after the funeral especially when someone has lost a spouse or child. Our Bereavement Team calls the family after the funeral to offer condolences again and to invite them to the bereavement workshops and sessions the parish offers. We immediately sense who needs more frequent calls and/or visits. A month after the funeral, the parish sends the bereaved a red rose and Mass card along with a letter of condolences. It is greatly appreciated.

Special Masses

Every three months a special evening Mass is offered for all who have died during that time. Invitations are sent to the families. It is always a very moving experience. Everyone present feels their grief very deeply, but the presence of others who mourn helps them to begin to reach out and minister to each other. It is very powerful.

During the memorial of the deceased at the Eucharistic Prayer, *everyone* lights a candle with the flame from the Paschal candle as the name of the loved one is read by the priest. It is so important for them to hear the names of their loved ones and know that they are not forgotten. Gestures like this are never forgotten by the families. That the parish cared about them in the time of their pain and loss will always be cherished.

Feast of All Souls

A similar type of Mass with the reading of all the names of the deceased of the past year is celebrated on All Souls' Day. People come in great numbers to remember their loved ones. With a little bit of planning and creativity a parish is able to make these events, which can be ordinary and predictable, into very moving and touching experiences that families remember and cherish for years to come.

At Home With the Lord

At Christmastime we place in the sanctuary a simple manger with a Christ Child that is made from soft doll-like materials. We invite our people to take the babe and hold it and rock it in their arms. This has proved to be a beautiful gesture for holding, healing and loving the injured child within the person. It is also a tender way to pray for a child who has died. People who have had abortions also have found this to be a moving way to pray for an aborted child as well as a way for praying for forgiveness and reconciliation.

Yes, we took a risk in doing this. But what has happened in quiet moments in the church as people held the child, rocked it and wept made the risk well worth it. Holding and touching and rocking prove to be very powerful means of healing.

Chapter Twelve

Creating Liturgies That Work

Most of our attempts to create community are not terribly creative; we simply use the celebrations and sacraments the Church has given us in the Ritual and Missal and add a few flourishes. *How* we use them is what matters!

One can attend a liturgically perfect Mass or celebration where everything is done by the book and you almost fall asleep. These celebrations lack a basic ingredient: passion. The rites of the Church are not meant to be celebrated in a sterile way. They have to be used intelligently as a servant of worship, not as the master. They should be the springboard of creativity, evangelization, healing and reconciliation. So many priests and liturgical teams and ministers are afraid to use their imagination and creativity and they become shackled to lifeless form and boring celebrations. For them the liturgical books are the "rule" books rather than the springboard to life-giving events that speak to and touch God's people. As Fr. Mike Maffeo would say, the books are the *terminus a quo,* not the *terminus ad quem.*

No one has all the gifts and talents. That's why Liturgy Committees help in providing a pool of ideas. By working together they create a year of grace and celebration. The team looks for many and varied opportunities to celebrate life and to lead God's people in prayer to experience the God who dwells in them.

There are so many wonderful ways to involve both adults and children in planning and celebrating events. It takes time, patience and hard work, but it's well worth it. It's the difference between living celebrations or routine observances. Every parish has the talent and the gifts to make the liturgy and all that accompanies it exciting, reverent, life-giving and a deep experience of the living God. If leaders give the people permission to think and use their talents, the parish will never be the same again.

The Pastoral Team must be willing to be creative and innovative with new liturgical and para-liturgical celebrations as well as with using the old treasures of the Church. Benediction, exposition, processions, May crownings, blessings, Tenebrae, morning and evening prayer, etc., are beautiful opportunities for preaching and teaching. All the traditional devotions can be used for the teaching of social justice themes and community responsibilities. We are not suggesting a proliferation of just *"me and Jesus"* devotions, rather *"Jesus and us and the world."*

In the years leading to and immediately after Vatican II, the liturgical movement was the call to life and liberty and joy in the Church. It became very closely associated with Peace and Justice issues. As we began to really celebrate and understand the Eucharist, the responsibility of sharing our bread and life with the poor became obvious. The liturgy was exciting and life-giving.

Unfortunately, the liturgy has become the moral theology of the Post Conciliar Days. In the past, moral theology measured and decreed every ounce of food one could *legitimately* eat during Lent. We even knew how long a kiss had to be for it to become a mortal sin! Law and order reigned.

Liturgy should be the expression of the freedom and joy of God's people. Parishes have to make liturgy the work of the people and the servant of the people. For the most part our liturgies are designed for middle aged, white and "well-off" people. Such people are wonderful (except for the "well-off" part, I'm right there), but we are not the whole Church.

Liturgy has to touch and serve the young and the old, the rich and the poor, all ethnic groups. Liturgy has to lead all people to an experience of God. If a person doesn't experience God's love and gentle mercy in the liturgy, that liturgy has not served the person well. If the cumulative effect of Mass Sunday after Sunday is boredom, aloofness, irrelevancy and esoteric celebrations that don't touch our hearts, our faith weakens and we begin to ask the questions: Why bother coming? What am I getting out of this? Thanks be to God most of our people are patient. But unless we create with them meaningful experiences of God, Mass will be reduced to a weekly obligation that one must get out of the way.

Remember that beautiful story in Matthew where he talks about the householder who brings out of his treasure both the old and the new *(Mt 13:51)*. When we reverence our past, no one fears the future. When we celebrate the present, everyone reverences the past. As we step into tomorrow we stand on the firm footing of yesterday and today.

The "Six"

We have tried to tailor Sunday Masses to the needs of the community. We celebrate in several languages. We have a lively family Mass, a choir Mass and even a quiet Mass at 6:30 A.M. The rock Mass begun by Fr. John White has been a real winner. It draws the youth, but also families and many who love the lively beat and message of the rock group.

The rock Mass is another way for the Church to say to our young people that they are also important to the life of the Church. The teen RAP (Religion and People) groups and Youth Retreat groups relate well with the rock Mass and the Youth Council that directs it. All of these activities together say that the young people are important. They also give the parish a youthful image which is very beneficial.

I cannot say it too often, A community loves the parish to reach out to children, teenagers and young adults. If you're good to my kids, you must be good!

Creating the Special Moments

As powerful and healing as the liturgical celebrations of the parish are, and as much as they truly build community, they are not enough. For community to grow in a parish the people have to have the opportunity of being together just to be together. Leadership has to create moments when we come together just to "waste time" and enjoy one another's company.

Fellowship after Mass is one of the best opportunities just "to be" together. Family Life Committees in parishes can plan many and varied social activities for couples and families that are inexpensive and fun. What builds family better than laughter and fun together? These are critical moments for the staff to be part of the celebration and joy. If I only pray with you but never play with you, then there's something wrong. It means I work *for* you but do not belong *to* you. I'm not part of the family. I only lead it. I'm responsible for it but I'm not a part of it. I'm above it and removed from it. I am a cleric, but not a brother. In the following pages I will share some of the special moments we celebrate at St. Brigid's that were and are very crucial in the creation of that family that we all yearn for in our parishes.

Please remember that each parish has to create its own special ways of praying and playing. We are not the same. I hope that all the examples cited in this book will only be a beginning list of possibilities for your parish.

Learning How to Celebrate

The Eucharist is the celebration and the work of the whole community. The clergy, music ministers, lectors, servers and Eucharistic ministers are there to serve the community. The priest, deacon and music ministers must remember how vital their role is.

Celebrating the Eucharist and preaching are arts. They must be learned and developed as the years go by. To stand in *persona Christi* is a frightening responsibility that should produce great humility.

Every priest should have himself videotaped when he says Mass and he should view the film with someone in the acting and communication fields. What kind of presence is projected? How do we communicate with gestures? How do we proclaim the Word? Are we really praying? Do we seem to believe what we are doing? Where's the fire? Do we really look into the eyes of our people? Do we smile? Is it ritual done by the book or is it deep sincere prayer of the heart led by one who deeply loves those with whom he celebrates the mystery of the Lord's death and resurrection?

Few of us are naturals, but we can all learn and we can all mature in our ability to lead public worship. There are many workshops and seminars offered on celebrating and preaching.

Preaching is the most important thing priests and deacons do. All the Adult Ed courses in the parish do not come near to the power and the potential of the preached word to touch the hearts of the people.

The most important ingredient in preaching is passion. It is so exciting to see the way someone acts and speaks when they are in love. They can't get enough of the beloved and they can't stop talking about the one they love.

Preaching is nothing more than sharing the flame of love that one has for Jesus. The preacher must be obviously in love and eager to share this treasure. Is that our experience of preaching? Is that how you preach? We can become better preachers, but it involves humility. It means giving someone permission to be totally honest by asking them: "Did my preaching bring you closer to Jesus?" What an opener that question is to begin to learn how to preach.

Courses and seminars help a lot in homily preparation but they tend to be esoteric and boring by concentrating on the content rather than the feeling behind it. The bottom line should always be, Did you share with your sisters and brothers the Jesus you know and love so well?

The Church must also recognize that the gift of preaching is not limited to the ordained and should try to create opportunities for the people to preach and tell their stories. Recently our dear Bishop John McGann invited married couples to preach in response to his pastoral letter on marriage. The results were overwhelmingly positive. Doesn't it make sense for the experts on a subject to speak about it?

Chapter Thirteen

We Celebrate the Mystery: From the Incarnation to the Resurrection

Flesh of Our Flesh — Advent

During Advent the Church proclaims the mystery of the Incarnation. Christ took flesh in time and He continues to take flesh in the lives of His sisters and brothers today. We *are* the Incarnation. As we look back to the joy of the Lord's birth in Bethlehem we also expect and celebrate His birth in each one of us at Advent and Christmas.

Advent is a very significant time of the year to stress the holiness of family life and relationships. It is the perfect time to lead families to claim their holiness and their beauty by reflecting on the life and family of Jesus.

Remember, it is our task to remind our people that they already have *everything*. Their holiness is to live out their relationships with great love and fidelity. The Church doesn't make our people holy; it reminds them of what is holy — their commitments, relationships and love.

The more the Church stresses the meaning and the holiness of family life, the more this holy time becomes the new incarnation of God's people living out their identity.

One of the best ways of creating the true spirit of Christmas is to have the children present a Christmas pageant. To hear the Christmas story told through one's children and grandchildren is true evangelization. The pageant is a truly successful way of welcoming many home in a very gentle and non-threatening way.

Of course, all the children who show up are in the pageant. We have many shepherds and shepherdesses, wise persons, and loads of angels. It's one of the best days of the year. It is always followed by fellowship during which the welcome continues and Santa pays a visit.

A concert is also a fine Advent activity for the families. People *love* to see their children perform, especially when it is in Church at the holiday season.

In all of these events the thrust is to honor the family and to help parents see that they are the present day Incarnation. Christ is born in their family by the love they have for one another. That love and service is their sanctity. Their love is what makes the Church holy. Why do so few of our people know that?

Christmas

The two family Masses we celebrate on Christmas Eve (4:00 P.M. and 5:30 P.M.) are among the most crowded of the whole year. They are packed with families, many of whom never go to church during the year. You have to give them the very best you have. The spirit of love and welcome has to fill the church — no wisecracks about not seeing them 'til next Easter allowed!

The parish must create a beautiful and loving Christmas Eve Mass for these families. We usually have the children act out the Gospel in costume (left over from the pageant). Our children's choir sings and as a special treat, Santa visits and shares the sermon with Father.

We make Santa a believer and worshipper of Jesus, just like the shepherds — *not* an enemy. We draw out from the exchange how Santa gives gifts to celebrate the greatest of all gifts — Jesus our Savior. Parents are very grateful for the help in resolving the Jesus/Santa conflict.*

Midnight Mass along with all the other Masses needs giant doses of welcome, patience, love and tenderness. They *are* our family even if they don't come regularly. Have we ever tried to figure out why we get so angry with non-churchgoers? Isn't it great that they are there twice a year? Let's say something beautiful and powerful so that they know they are loved and that they are always welcome. Let's not fall into the trap of equating holiness with attendance at Mass. Let's rather create a Church and liturgy where people are drawn because they truly experience the power of the love of Jesus and His Body.

It is a much appreciated act of kindness to send each household a Christmas card from the Church staff. It is a card sharing love to a member of the family assuring them they will be remembered in all the Christmas Masses. Don't send it with the schedule mailing or the Christmas fund appeal. Send it the way an individual sends a friend a Christmas card.

New Year's Eve and Day

We gather people together on New Year's Eve for a special Mass for peace at 11:00 P.M. This Mass is preceded by Exposition of the Blessed Sacrament following the 5:00 P.M. Mass. This candlelight Mass is followed by a champagne toast in the rectory. Many people have nowhere to go on New Year's Eve and it's nice to offer them some fellowship.

On New Year's Day the principal Mass is a multi-cultural celebration. Although the American Bishops have done all in their power to minimize it and the other Holy Days (under the premise that going to Mass two days in a row when it

---

*The complete dialogue between Santa and the priest can be found in Part III of this book and in *What Shall I Give Him Poor As I Am?* by Francis X. Gaeta.

falls on a Monday is an unbearable burden); most of our people don't think so. People like to begin the new year with Mass. They are not going because of the Solemnity of Mary on World Peace Day; they are going because it's good luck and good sense and basically sound theology to begin a new venture, like a new year, with Mass. But what would the people know about something like that!

Things like new beginnings and resolutions may not appeal to the very religious and intellectual, but the opportunity to make new beginnings with God's blessings is very important and much appreciated by ordinary people. To encourage such positive behavior should be one of the great objectives of religion. In many cases it seems to be what the establishment delights in undermining.

The Presepio

For eight years a team of our parishioners has constructed what we call the Presepio during Advent/Christmas. It's an Italian word for a very elaborate scene that presents the Nativity in a local town scene. Our Presepio now contains over two hundred figures. It is created and added to each year as an act of faith and love — the second generations of families are already learning the ropes.

We use it as a wonderful tool of evangelization for our children and also for adults who come from all over to visit and to pray. During the Advent phase, Mary and Joseph make their way through the town — Bethlehem/Westbury/Rocky Point — *your town.* The townspeople do not know the reality that the Lord is passing among us waiting for us to recognize Him.

The Presepio is a work of art. It is an expression of deep faith on the part of the dedicated team. It is also the means to renew the faith and love of the people of the parish and the hundreds who come to visit.

Living Nativity

On the grounds of the church we set up a life-size Nativity. It is the destination of many of the processions we have in late Advent and Christmas to Bethlehem. These processions are always followed by fellowship.

As I mentioned earlier in Chapter 9, on the Feast of the Baptism of the Lord all the babies baptized in the previous year are invited back. They are invited to "stand in" for Baby Jesus who is today surrounded by live animals.

We Fast and We Feast

Lent and Easter are very special times in which most people feel drawn to the Lord and will do or give up something. It is a time for the Church to offer opportunities for prayer, good works and education to its people. The traditional devotions of Stations of the Cross, evening Masses, Exposition of the Blessed Sacrament, etc., all enhance the spirit of Lent and of entering into the mystery of the death and resurrection of the Lord.

We stress the theme of Lent being the time to feast and a time to fast. We feast *on* very positive things like love, forgiveness, the mercy of God, healing, reconciliation, etc. We fast *from* negative things like anger, laziness, negativity, prejudice, etc. This *twist* in the usual fasting message can help to create a much more positive and healthy Lenten Season that leads us naturally to the great celebration of the Lord's Resurrection.

Ash Wednesday

Most parish staffs dread Ash Wednesday. The thought of hordes of the unwashed and unchurched leads some to swooning. Why are we keeping these semi-pagan rituals alive? Why are we even interested in the non-practicing, non-paying people? This seems to be the day when we look down our noses at the rabble and by Church body language, or even by our words, (A & P Catholics!) we tell them to get lost. (Of course, we do this just as our Protestant sisters and brothers are re-discussing the power of sign and sacrament and re-introducing ashes *back* into their services.)

Ash Wednesday has the possibility of being one of the really beautiful days in the Church year. It's all up to the staff, especially the clergy and liturgical ministers. We have to communicate welcome and love and our delight that so many of our people are with us. We have to preach from our heart to all of our dear people. There is *always* someone just waiting for you to call them home.

After thirty-three years as a priest I have only recently learned how to give out ashes. I look at the person and I smile. I pray the formula which goes something like this: "Believe in the Good News. Accept Jesus with all your heart. He loves you so much!" After I trace the cross on the person's forehead, I lay my hands on their head in prayer and then I give them a gentle caress on the cheek, like the sign of peace the bishop used to give at Confirmation. In the few seconds more that this takes I (the Church, Christ) have touched in love a sister/brother. People don't forget signs of love.

The beauty of the Scriptures, music, decorations and above all the preaching can make this a most memorable moment for our people. Of course, there will be people you won't see for another year, but there will be others who will begin to think about their love affair with Jesus and they will begin to come closer. Even those who don't return for another year will be touched in some way.

Perhaps the person who is suffering from AIDS or is HIV positive won't come back right now, but she/he will at least feel that the Church is the place where they will be loved and not condemned. That goes for the person who had an abortion and is too ashamed to believe in God's love for them. It goes for all those bearing heavy burdens. The list is endless.

All I know is that on Ash Wednesday we see in our churches people we never see at any other time. Do we give them our best? Or are we, the self-righteous elite, annoyed at the lack of faith of these people? We need to ask ourselves what Jesus would do. How would Jesus treat the least of His brothers and sisters? Let's pick up the Gospels and prepare for Ash Wednesday by reading about how Jesus spent the equivalent of His own Ash Wednesdays. Chapter 14 in the Gospel of Luke would be a great scripture to pray over before Ash Wednesday.

It's good to provide more opportunities for Mass and services on Ash Wednesday. If you do, more and more people will come. We all *belong* in church on this day. It's good to advertise in your local newspapers. Advertising (evangelization) says to the world, "*We* believe in this stuff and we are delighted to have you come join us!" Don't underestimate the good you can do with a little prayer, preparation and common sense. Ignore the crepehangers and the negativity you may meet. If you're reaching out to God's people, you're right! If you really reach out you will see beautiful results.

Another thought on Ash Wednesday: plan something very special for the kids. They love to get ashes. They love to give something up. Help them to find their Jesus and respect their beautiful religious instincts. They *want* to do something special. Also give out something tangible — nails, crosses, hearts, stones, etc. People *love* to carry something with them to remind them of Ash Wednesday. Give them a bit of homework for prayer and reflection. Spend some money on a booklet of prayers or reflections for each day of Lent. Families love to read them together at supper time. (I know of two such great booklets, one for Advent and one for Lent authored by yours truly!)

There are many parishes where these kinds of things are taking place all the time. What a blessing they are to the Church. Your parish can do the same. Start off easy and build a little more each year. That's how community grows. But again the basic questions have to be asked: Do we want community or an efficient machine? Do we want to distribute ashes or embrace the family? Are we willing to pay the price for community?

On this Ash Wednesday when you face the hordes of people looking for ashes, think of Jesus as He faced the shore of the Sea of Galilee. Jesus looked at His people with love and spoke the first word of the Sermon on the Mount, "Blessed." Our people *are* blessed; they are holy. They are waiting for someone like you to welcome them in the love of Jesus and to share their lives with them. They don't want or need a bureaucrat or cleric to look down his/her nose on them in disgust. They didn't want or need that when Jesus invited them into His open air church and they don't today when we welcome them in the name of Jesus in our churches. They responded then to someone who loved them so much that He gave his life for them. It made sense then and it makes sense now. That's all that will ever work.

Someday, the Church will canonize the great genius who first celebrated Ash Wednesday along with all the parish secretaries who for the zillionth time (and with a smile) tell Mrs. Jones what time the ashes are being distributed. And please, for God's sake, give the ashes to babies and children and by all means put some in the tissue for Tony to take home to his wife! Amen! Ash Wednesday is one of the Lord's greatest gifts. Use it well.

The Passion Play

In the same way that the Christmas Pageant touches our children and adults, so does the annual Passion Play presented by our children. The same holy effect is achieved as our children preach the touching message of the Lord's Passion and Death. The acting, music and dancing of our beloved children can touch the most hardened hearts. When we allow our children to minister to us, powerful things happen to the children and to us.

All of these family/children events can happen when the Family Life Committee owns the project and organizes it and works on it each year. There are plenty of good and dedicated adults who are willing to do the work to make these events possible. Remember, the more a parish does for its kids, the more adults will love the parish *and* support it. If you love my kids you love *me!*

Tenebrae

We have adapted the ancient service of Tenebrae (shadows or darkness) as a meaningful evening prayer service. The service centers around the lighting and extinguishing of fifteen candles on a large candelabra called the hearse. One of our saints exquisitely hand-crafted ours, modeling it on the one we borrowed from our diocesan seminary.

The service is very serious and solemn and speaks to a very special group. We make the Tenebrae the occasion of having guest speakers. The preaching usually touches on a Peace and Justice theme that flows from our meditation on the Passion of Jesus.

A special team of lay ministers have been trained and are now responsible for Tenebrae. They, in turn, train the celebrant and all lay participants, numbering about twelve for each evening. The team owns it and they do a wonderful job in presenting another opportunity for prayer during Lent.

Parish Retreats

Lent and Christmas are natural times for providing the special prayer experience of a week long parish retreat/mission. Care must be taken to ensure that the preachers are sound and will deepen and enhance the spirit of the parish. I find that we get our best leads by word of mouth.

During these retreats all the other parish meetings and prayer groups should shut down. Everyone must be encouraged to go to the retreat sessions. The clergy and staff should also make every effort to be present at the services. Their presence speaks volumes about how important these events are in the life of a parish.

The Seder

We celebrate the Seder meal close to Holy Week. It not only helps us to understand our Jewish roots and spirituality but gives us a deeper appreciation and love of our Jewish friends and neighbors. We are constantly teaching about the evil of sexism, anti-Semitism, racism, homosexual bashing and all the other evils that are present in the world today. If we at St. Brigid's with all of our colors, languages, nationalities, religions and economically diverse people can love one another, then the whole world can. That is our mission. That is your mission. Each parish is a tiny part of the kingdom and a place where Jesus reigns and love is spoken.

Our Fr. Marty Klein is a convert from Judaism. His presence is a special grace. He inspires us to be open, loving and welcoming to people of all other faiths, from Jewish people and Protestants to Muslims. There is, after all, only one God and Father of us all. The more the Church cherishes and respects other faiths, the more powerful and believable the Gospel we preach becomes.

The Catholic Mosaic: Holy Thursday

Many of our parishes are becoming multi-cultural. The response to that at the beginning of this century was to establish ethnic or national parishes. Today the Church in our area seems to prefer the multi-cultural parish. It brings great challenges but also great blessings to a parish. At St. Brigid's we have Mass in Spanish, Creole, Italian and English each and every Sunday. Several times during the year we celebrate multi-cultural Masses and other celebrations to bring the whole community together and to give us the privilege of worshipping in the languages and customs of our sisters and brothers. It is a tremendous challenge and an incredible amount of work. We could never do it without the services of a full time liturgist, organist and director of music. The parish is staffed with one priest, Fr. Tom Costa, who is fluent in many languages but the rest of us are at least able to say Mass in the other languages with a lot of help from God's people.

Our greatest multi-cultural celebration is the Mass of the Lord's Supper on Holy Thursday Evening. We celebrate at the school gym almost a mile away from the church. The liturgy planning committee arranges a glorious celebration including the Washing of the Feet. This celebration uses all of our languages and music traditions. After Mass we process by candlelight to the church through the streets of the parish with the Blessed Sacrament. A portable PA system allows us to praise the Lord and evangelize the community. What a great sight it is to see the patrons of the bars and pizzerias come out to look and pray!

The arrival at the church is glorious. The church is packed with people when we welcome the Lord in beautiful and loving song. The main altar is gloriously decorated as the Altar of Repose for the Blessed Sacrament by our Hispanic Community. The consecrated Body and Blood is placed upon the altar and parishioners worship the holy sacrament all night long. The sacrament is reposed and the altar decorations taken down after the 9:00 A.M. Morning Prayer on Good Friday.

Children's Holy Thursday and Good Friday

On Holy Thursday morning we have a special Mass of the Lord's Supper for our children. At the Washing of the Feet, the parents and families are invited to bring their children into the sanctuary where there are stations for parents and clergy together to wash the children's feet. What a moving scene that is. Parents are always serving the way Jesus did.

On Good Friday we have a special service during which the parents bring their children into the sanctuary and hold the crucifix for the children to kiss or hug or just touch it. How moving that veneration of the crucifix is for everyone in the church — most of all the parents.

On both days the preacher stresses the holiness of parenting and that it is the family that leads us to Jesus. For it is in the family where we touch and love one another that we first touch and love Jesus.

At the conclusion of the children's Holy Thursday Mass we process with the Blessed Sacrament on the grounds of the church. The Blessed Sacrament is exposed until 4:00 P.M. Senior Citizens and young children who cannot get out at night appreciate the opportunity to make a visit and adore the Lord in the Blessed Sacrament. (The parish has exposition every Thursday afternoon all year long and it is well attended.)

At the end of the Mass and procession the Gazebo-ettes (our dedicated ministers of hospitality so named after our hospitality center on St. Brigid's Green — St. Martha's Gazebo) provide us with matzos (great with cream cheese!) and grape juice.

If we do not celebrate these days with our children, will they ever learn of our rich and blessed tradition? It *is* a lot of work to do these extra things during Holy Week, but what will happen if we do *not* do them?

Good Friday

You will see from the section on Holy Week in Part III that we never stop on Good Friday. Good Friday is *the* day that people want to come to church. We provide varied and different prayer opportunities. In addition to the solemn liturgies for adults and children, we are blessed with outdoor processions and the Stations of the Cross dramatized by our Italian and Hispanic communities. They are very moving and well attended by all of our people.

We also have the Living Stations of the Cross presented by our young adults in the church at 8:00 P.M. The acting, dancing and contemporary bent to the narration draws a huge crowd and always packs the church.

As the Stations of the Cross come to an end in the church, the Christus character is carried out. At the same time the procession with the statue of the Dead Christ—Jesus Sepultado—arrives at the church. The statue is carried into the packed church and is greeted by hymns and prayers. It is a very emotional moment. All reverence the statue. It is one of these moments when our Hispanic parishioners give "permission" to all of us to feel and show our emotions. The whole church gathers around the bier of Christ like a family sharing the pain and loss of the Lord. We support and strengthen one another in our faith and love.

Seven Last Words

From noon to three o'clock we present the Service of the Seven Last Words of Christ. We have put together a beautiful devotion for the Three Hours enhanced by the preaching of seven parishioners on Jesus' seven last words. It has proven to be a very moving and intense way for many people to spend Good Friday. Word spreads and the crowds grow each year. There is a power we are only beginning to tap, when we invite our people to tell their story in the context of the words of Jesus.

Holy Saturday

Holy Saturday is a quiet day of preparation for the Great Vigil of Easter. During the day a statue of the Dead Christ (Jesus Sepultado) lies in state. In the morning the final confessions are heard.

People come all day. They touch the statue and kiss it and caress it. It is a real wake. Our Hispanic parishioners have given us permission to feel and to express our faith and it's wonderful! There's no going back for the community of St. Brigid's.

At 4:00 P.M. we pray the final prayer before the vigil — a sort of Mid-Day Prayer. This year there were over one hundred people at that prayer service. Believe me, they all went to Easter Mass, too!

Blessing of the Foods

On Holy Saturday after the Morning Prayer we invite our parishioners to place food for their Easter table on the altar to be blessed. This means so much to people from Poland and other Eastern European countries. It has grown over the years and has become another celebration of family life. An unanticipated bonus has become the delicious ethnic baked goods the people bring for Father! When I get to heaven I'm going to ask Jesus how He kept the weight off with all His table ministry!

The Great Vigil of Easter

We celebrate as fully as possible the great night. It takes a long time (four hours). A parish joke is to ask if the Vigil is over yet.

The baptisms and reception of the new members is at the heart of the Vigil. So many people participate in the preparation and the planning. It truly becomes a night of celebrating who we are as we embrace new family members.

A great help in bringing a whole new understanding to your Easter Vigil is the video *This Is the Night! A Parish Welcomes New Members* by Liturgy Training Publications published by the Archdiocese of Chicago. The RCIA team, choirs and liturgy committee should work together to make this night the night of nights. There are nights like Holy Saturday when you have to put the clock away and really celebrate the new life that Christ gives us. Celebrate it and enjoy it!

Every member of the parish involved in ministry is sent a picture of one of the candidates on the First Sunday of Lent.

They are asked to pray for them and to come to the vigil to celebrate their entrance into our Church family.

The Risen Christ and the Tomb

This year at the suggestion of a certain pastor, a new team constructed a beautiful scene of the empty tomb. At its center they placed a powerful life-sized statue of the Risen Christ. It is constructed in the same place as the Presepio. It becomes a beautiful, quiet prayer and meditation place for the people.

The Tomb Team has flowered and grown like the Presepio Team. They took an idea and ran with it. They, too, did a beautiful job. It is already becoming intergenerational. Also, like the Presepio, the parishioners and visitors come from all over to marvel and admire the faith and skill of the holy people who created it.

During the time outside Advent, Christmas and Easter, a beautiful, life-sized crucifix rests on the wall. All year long people come to look, to think, to weep and to pray there.

Easter Sunrise

We gather on Easter morning at the beach before sunrise and celebrate a glorious Liturgy of the Resurrection based on the Easter Vigil. It has become a tradition for the priest celebrant to go out into the Atlantic Ocean to fill a jug with ocean water for the blessing of the people and the renewal of the Baptismal Promises. Each person also receives a piece of wood on which we write our sins for the new fire.

The joy and laughter and cold along with the faith of these beautiful people create a moment in Church life that is unique and sacramental. No one ever forgets the scene of the parish lunatics led by the clergy and staff (wrapped up and shivering) praising and glorifying the risen Lord.

Memories are such a holy and gentle grace. We know there is love in a community when our memories are filled with images of a joyful, laughing (and at times crying) family that has shared a moment of time together that will last forever. The more we can do that, the more we know that we have been part of something greater than ourselves — a family!

There were sixty people present at our first sunrise experience in 1990. In 1995 there were 1,200 people present. Yes, we do have our regular Easter collection! It does take a special team to organize and plan the Easter dawn activities. Please don't ever gather a thousand people at the beach in the dark without being well organized. It would be a disaster.

We haven't yet worked out a way to have fellowship for all those people. Who knows what next year will bring? The "gazeboettes" are never conquered! They'll find a way!

Easter Sunday

Where do they come from? What a collection! The crowds are huge, but not even half of our people come at Easter or any other time. What a job we have to do for the Lord!

On Easter Sunday, the same principles apply as on Christmas. We welcome our beautiful families with love, warmth, sincerity and genuine affection. They deserve nothing less and the Lord demands nothing less.

On Easter we work very hard as His unworthy servants giving our hearts and souls to all who come to us. It is in that love that new life will definitely come to us and it is in that love that new life may also come to these beloved sisters and brothers. And remember, we can rest up during Easter week.

Spring Liturgy

We continue the joy of the Easter celebration the Sunday after Easter. The 1:00 P.M. Mass that day becomes the Family Mass and the Family Life Team plans a special liturgy to continue our catechesis with children and adults on the mystery of the Lord's Resurrection and our life together in Jesus.

The Gospel and homily will include a skit on Easter by the

children with special music provided by our beautiful children's choir. The Mass comes to a close with a loud knock on the wall. The celebrant responds: "Who could that be boys and girls?" None other than Miss E. Bunny appears to the delight of all. She embraces Father wishing him a "Happy Easter." Miss E. Bunny and Father then lead everyone outside to the St. Brigid's Green where a great family festival takes place.

Diego is there with his pony rides and petting zoo. There is face painting by clowns, a few rides for the kids, hot dogs, popcorn, balloons, games and activities. In short, it is a time when the parish simply enjoys being together to have some fun and to enjoy one another. It is a lot of hard work for the Family Life Team, but it works and it again makes the Sacrament of Community very real and very meaningful for many families. It costs almost nothing, but its value goes on and on.

Once you feel you are part of something, once you believe you belong, the spirit of love, unity and reconciliation grows stronger and stronger and nothing can stop it.

Community just doesn't happen. It takes constant planning and work. The parish must do things well and it must do them consistently. We have to strive for excellence, not perfection, in everything we do. We learn from our mistakes; we improve, adapt and adjust; but we never give up or allow ourselves the luxury of complacency.

The Vigil of Pentecost

We use all the options of readings and prayers to create a beautiful Vigil of Pentecost. We again bless the fire of the Holy Spirit outside the church and renew our Baptism promises by candlelight. We pray for the coming of the Holy Spirit upon all present.

The most moving thing we do for Pentecost is to have the new Catholics who were baptized and received into the Church at the Easter Vigil give the homily for the evening as a faith sharing about their journey to the Church and their conversion.

Afterward we celebrate at St. Martha's Gazebo and continue our welcoming of the new Catholics. People are so proud of them and delight at the opportunity to welcome them and hear their stories.

The Pentecost Vigil is growing each year because people look to celebrate and pray for the coming of the Holy Spirit. Again it results from using the treasures the Church has given to us. The readings, fire, candles, holy water, renewal of promises, all of these elements are at our disposal. The only real innovative aspect (and the most important) is the testimony of our new Catholics. I cannot overemphasize how moving it is for the whole community to hear why people have become Catholics. It is a magnificent conclusion to all the public rites of Lent and Holy Week.

Chapter Fourteen

We Celebrate All Year

Labor Day

The real New Year's Day for parishes is not the First Sunday of Advent or January 1. It's Labor Day! Vacations are over, the kids go back to school and parishes begin to gear up for a New Year of work and play.

We note the beginning of the New Year with a special Mass on Labor Day in honor of St. Joseph the Worker. The parish gathers outside by Our Lady's statue for some Introductory Rites. We introduce ourselves to one another, dedicate the year to our Lady and move to the portals of the church. The pastor strikes the portals with the hand-carved parish staff. The doors are opened by couples who are expecting a child along with their other children. They welcome us to God's house and we follow them to the altar.

These same families will do the readings, dress the altar and say a few words about the big Church and the little Church.

After Mass we have a wonderful breakfast on the church Green and also draw the winning tickets for the Summer Maintenance Raffle and the Dinner at the Rectory for the Bishop's Annual Appeal Drive.

The beginning of the year brings us together in a joyful mode and it reminds us of how beautiful and sacramental our work is. People must have a sense of the sacred in their work.

This special liturgy and the Sunday Masses on Labor Day weekend are a very fine way to remind one another that we build the Kingdom of God by our labors. Because of the Incarnation our work and labor are very sacred and very precious. If the Church is not constantly reminding its people what the Incarnation means in their daily lives it is failing and cheating them of the gift of life and meaning that the Lord wants them to enjoy.

Labor Day, like so many other events in the parish life, celebrates the goodness of our people and reminds them that they are the Lord's saints. The Church can do no greater service to its people and to the whole world than continuously reminding them of their identity as children of God. The holiness we have all been called to is to live our lives and vocations with all our hearts and souls. Our sanctity is our identity. What a privilege it is for the Church, especially its preachers and teachers, to remind God's people of their exalted call and to be there to help them to celebrate it.

Feast of St. Francis of Assisi – October 4

The main celebration of the St. Francis Feast Day is the blessing of animals on St. Brigid's Green. People love their pets. They are best friends to many people. So on the feast of Francis, the cats and dogs, hamsters and snakes, fish and birds, horses and all the others come to be blessed in the spirit and love of that holy man of Assisi who taught us that all creation is part of our family and that we are all inter-related.

The blessing includes a procession around the church grounds of all the animals led by a beautiful police horse with Officer Jim astride. It's a delight to behold. The "happy hour" at the Green continues the celebration of life, love, family and friends. Everyone receives a copy of the Prayer of St. Francis to take home to remember the day and the animals and the good and loving God who saw that it was all *very* good.

Our Lady of Guadalupe – December 12

We have been celebrating a yearly multi-cultural Mass and celebration in honor of Mary the Patroness of the Americas and the symbol of our devotion to life. This celebration of Our Lady honors all the countries of Central and South America. Each country is different, has varied customs and a great variety of wonderful foods. All these things are celebrated in the liturgy and the festive party that follows. Hispanic people come from all over to honor Mary and to be reminded of home through the music and food. What an incredible privilege the Church has in being able to gather together so many people to be family and friends. The Church is their real home away from home. What a holy thing we are part of. Let's really do a good job in welcoming the stranger.

So many of us can tell horror stories of how terribly our ancestors were treated by the Church and society when they came to the United States. The Irish, Italian, Poles, Germans, etc., were treated with prejudice and coldness by the "established" group. The tragedy is that each group treated the newest groups as badly, if not worse, than they had been treated. We at St. Brigid's are working hard to end the cycle of hate and prejudice and replacing it with the kingdom of love and welcome that Jesus taught. Our former pastor, Fr. Fred Schaefer, made the rectory and the parish a place of welcome for everyone. We are trying to continue what that saint began.

Thanksgiving Day

This holiday is a magnificent celebration. We celebrate a 9:00 A.M. multi-cultural liturgy. Everyone is there. The place is packed. The theme always centers around thanking God for the blessing of one another. It is so moving to see the whole family together thanking the Lord for the gift of our unity in diversity. You just can't get more American or Catholic than that!

Thanksgiving Day is a holy opportunity to remind all our immigrants (beginning in 1850 and still going on as of last week) of the sacred words of Emma Lazarus in her poem, *New Colossus* for the Statue of Liberty:

Give me your tired, your poor
your huddled masses yearning to breathe free,
The wretched refuse of your teeming shore.
Send these, the homeless, tempest-tost to me.
I lift my lamp beside the golden door!

Remember, every liturgy in some way should celebrate the dignity and rights of each person. Just like Jesus, the Church will always be comforting the afflicted and afflicting the comfortable. That's liturgy! In the normal scope of parish life and liturgy, the Church will be consistently preaching the rights of the unborn, the homeless, the homosexual, the immigrant. The Church speaks against mercy killings and the death penalty and war. The parish is the place where these values must be preached and defended. If not in the parish, then where?

Feast of St. Blase – February 4

The Feast of St. Blase and the blessing of throats presents another opportunity for the Church to touch her beloved people with prayers, healing and intercession. When a parish takes time and interest to celebrate days like St. Blase's Feast Day it is saying that it cares and that it *enjoys* being together with its people. It is very clear on this day how serious parents are about praying for the health and well-being of their children. The prayer of the Church and the ministry of the Church mean so much to the people. Unfortunately, we sometimes underestimate the faith and devotion of our people. As we dismiss days like the feast of St. Blase, we give away another opportunity to celebrate our love for our people and to pray with them.

St. Patrick – March 17

March 17 is a big deal at St. Brigid's! We celebrate a joyful Mass in his honor. We create a little Croagh Patrick in the sanctuary with him at the summit. He is surrounded by hundreds of little pots of shamrocks that are solemnly blessed and distributed to all the people after Mass. The shamrocks also adorn the altar and play into the homily in some way. I try to make the homily a bit of a Hal Roach special. Piper, green vestments, Irish music (*Danny Boy* and *The Fields of Athenry*), Gaelic readings, all add to a great celebration. After Mass, following the parish motto of "From Holy Hour to Happy Hour," we celebrate with good Irish music, Irish coffee and soda bread. The church and hall are packed.

San Giuseppe – March 19

March 19 follows with the same kind of glorious celebration in honor of St. Joseph. We bless and distribute St. Joseph's Bread in this wonderful Italian-English liturgy. Afterwards we go again from "you know what" to "you know what." This time the featured treat is *pasta con fagiola* and *cannoli* and *espresso with Zambuca*. It's wonderful! And no, you don't have to be Italian or Irish to be at these celebrations. Everybody comes. For St. Joseph's Day, Croagh Patrick, turns into Monte Giuseppe, as his statue replaces Patrick and the bread replaces the shamrocks. The more we affirm and celebrate the different parts of the Body, the more we celebrate ourselves and the wider world.

May Crowning

We have many processions through the streets of Westbury. We celebrate Corpus Christi, Holy Thursday, St. Anthony's Day and the Assumption in this way. The different groups organize their special processions all of which begin at church with Mass.

This year our Family Life and Religious Education Committees are preparing a May Procession and Crowning of Mary that is a little different. Our First Communion children will lead us in procession through the streets of our town with a marching band from Brooklyn at the head.

The children will carry a very large (45 foot) rosary. Each bead will be held by a child. We will stop at five special Marian shrines erected by a host family. At each of these shrines the children will lead us in praying the decades of the rosary. We will conclude the procession on the Green by crowning the Statue of Our Lady. After the ceremony, the famous Gazeboettes will offer some good Westbury refreshments to all.

This parish aspect of the faith is very healthy and again builds community. I'm very anxious to see how Our Lady's Day will work out. But let me give you a hint: There are fifty some beads on the rosary which means fifty some second graders in their First Communion outfits plus the Legion of Mary, the Rosary Society, etc., etc. Multiply that fifty-some by the parents, grandparents, sisters and brothers, all marching through the streets praying the rosary and you will have an idea of the possibilities!

It will, of course, take two indispensable words — work and planning. Without them you have chaos and disaster. With them you will have sincere, beautiful prayer, deepening of devotion to Our Lady and the building of memories and community.

Corpus Christi

On the feast of Corpus Christi we process through the streets of our town with the Blessed Sacrament to several altars (six) along the way. Each Benediction is ministered and prepared by a different ethnic and language group.

We begin with a multi-cultural Mass and then process with the Sacrament. Twelve representatives from all the communities are chosen to carry the canopy over the priests as they take turns carrying the Blessed Sacrament.

Our First Communion children and members of all the parish and town societies participate. It has grown to be a very significant event in our parish. Our Italian Community began the procession ten years ago and they have shared it with the whole community.

On many different levels, the feast of Corpus Christi enriches and deepens the faith life of the whole community and it fires the Catholic imagination and identity of which Fr. Andrew Greeley writes so beautifully.

St. Anthony – June 13

St. Anthony's Feast is very popular. He *is* people's favorite saint — or so they say. Our local St. Anthony Society in the village arranges a festive Eucharist which includes the blessing and distribution of St. Anthony's bread. St. Anthony is enthroned on top of the mountain of bread in the sanctuary just like St. Joseph. The church is packed for this one.

After Mass, the Society conducts a procession of the statue through the streets of the town, led by a fabulous marching band. It's a very pleasant June evening for all. The meatball and sausage and pepper heroes and homemade wine after the procession top off a perfect day!

The Real Feast Days

The Church has a calendar that sometimes doesn't jive with the real calendar of people. I've mentioned days like St. Patrick's Day, Valentine's Day, Labor Day, Thanksgiving Day, Ash Wednesday, that are very important to the people. There are other days and moments that the Church doesn't seem to understand and thus under-celebrates if not totally ignores. At St. Brigid's we are trying to celebrate what means a great deal to people — at the top of the list — Mother's Day and Father's Day.

Mother's Day

On this day every boy and girl has made their mom breakfast in bed. They have broken into their piggy banks (or borrowed from dad) to buy mom a present. Grown children in far-off places will call, send a card or take their mother out to dinner. Others will shed a tear or maybe stop at the cemetery. In other words, today is a big deal for almost everybody.

The official calendar of the Church, however, will warn us that the secular observance of Mother's Day should in no way diminish from the main focus of the Sunday of Easter, namely, the Paschal Mystery. Some mention of the "secular" feast may be made in the Prayer of the Faithful or the Prayer Over the People.

I cannot imagine how anything could ever more completely live out and celebrate the Paschal Mystery than motherhood (or fatherhood). The entire celebration should be geared to motherhood and family life. This is a wonderful day for mothers to preach!

At the Lord's Prayer we usually invite all the mothers to gather around the altar. As the Body and Blood of Christ is present on the altar these great women of God are reminded that as they look at their beloved children they can also say, "This is the Body of Christ." (Every child born into the world is the Christ Child!)

We all join hands around the altar and through the church as we say a special prayer of thanksgiving for these holy women who bring life into our world and Church. We then pray with these saints as we pray The Lord's Prayer.

The principle at work here is that the life of a loving mother is holy. It is sanctified. The Church's role is to affirm and remind these holy women who they are and what they give to the Church. What a blessing this is for the spouses of these women and their children as they pray with and for their wife/mother. Remember, if you honor, praise and recognize my mother, you give me the most wonderful gift I can ever receive. My mother is dead almost twenty years but when I meet her former students and they tell me how special she was to them, it brings a tear to my eye. It makes my day to know that someone appreciates and remembers my mother.

Imagine what it does to a young boy or girl to know how important and special their grandmother and mother are to the Church! Also, as a final gesture of our esteem, each mother, grandmother and godmother is presented with a flower as they leave church. On Mother's Day the bulletin will always contain some very special articles, tributes, prayers and poems about our mothers. After Mass the happy hour phase takes over to continue the party begun at the Eucharist.

On this day our prayers also go out to those who mourn the loss of a beloved mother and to mothers who, for whatever reason, couldn't be what we needed them to be. The greatest praise and love today is given to single mothers who faithfully and lovingly care for their families. They are the true saints of our Church. The Church has to let them know how holy and special they are to all of us.

Father's Day

All I can say about Father's Day is "ditto" to what I have said about Mother's Day. The liturgy and celebration is planned basically the same way, with one serious comment: the men need it even more.

So much of what kids see on TV today depicts fathers as imbeciles and simpletons. Even in the Church, despite the male monopoly on Holy Orders, men are becoming more and more peripheral members of the Church. The vast majority of all the work in the Church is done by women. Often the male priest is surrounded my almost all female servers, EM's, lectors and choir members and even ushers. Something is lacking in male participation and in male spirituality. Local parishes have to face this. Our men are not comfortable enough to come forth for ministry. It's not just a question of work. Many women work as many hours as men but they seem to have more interest, time and talent for ministry. Men really need to be ministered to in the Church today.

Women are the real ordained ministers of the Church. They do everything but say Mass. Men are becoming less involved in the real work of the Church while holding on to the power of sacramental ordination.

Father's Day is a very important opportunity to affirm men and fatherhood. It is an opportunity to call men back to their place in the Church. It is only the beginning, however. Parishes have to face this dilemma or they will become progressively unhealthy and lopsided.

As we said about motherhood, nothing could be a greater living out of the Paschal Mystery than fatherhood and being a good husband. The Church has to celebrate the holiness inherent in living this life in today's world. It is not easy as husband or wife, father or mother, to lay down one's life in love. It is truly saintly to do so — nothing less. Let the Church praise and glorify its holy men and women always, but especially on their day!

Jesus Evening

Every First Friday we celebrate a special charismatic healing Mass during which we pray over people. Before I outline the evening I will tell you why in my own opinion it is such a grace to the parish: all the priests have agreed to concelebrate, to take turns as celebrant/preacher, to hear confessions and to be part of the pray-over teams. Many parishioners have told me how moved they are to see their priests praying before the Blessed Sacrament at adoration. When the clergy are together in prayer, it gives a very powerful message to the people. In St. Brigid's it is a most powerful sign of our love and respect for one another and our love for our people.

This is the schedule for the Jesus Evening:

7:15 Music ministry begins time of praise and prayer

7:30 Evening's Leader leads more praise and prayer (members of the Prayer Group will share readings and prophecy)

7:45 Mass begins with an extended homily

9:00 Exposition of the Blessed Sacrament during which there are confessions and prayovers with Prayer Teams

10:00 Nocturnal Adoration Holy Hour

The purpose for the Jesus Evening is to dedicate an evening once a month to praise and worship Jesus. We make it His evening as a time of praise, adoration, petition and healing. The people are invited to come for all or a part of the evening. The evening is obviously very upbeat and it leans to the charismatic style but everyone is comfortable. People come from distant places for this Mass and to be prayed over. There is a tremendous need in the Church for this kind of personal and physical ministry. The Church should be the greatest toucher and hugger. The Church should be the greatest lover of all.

The Jesus Evening is an experience of very real, gentle Christian loving. The priest is probably the one to experience it the most as he receives the deep affirmation, appreciation and love of his people. Something like the Jesus Evening is worth all the time, planning and work it requires. None of these events will succeed without a lot of hard work. Our prayer group and music ministry make the evening happen.

Monday Evenings on the Green

Each summer, on the Mondays of August, we invite people together for Evening Prayer on the lawn of the church. We especially encourage families to come. Everyone brings a lawn chair or blanket. For an hour we praise the Lord together.

We have been blessed at St. Brigid's with a wonderful music group made up of members of the Filipino community. They are filled with joy and happiness. Their music radiates the love of Jesus. Everyone feels at home.

The warm-up music begins at 7:00 P.M. and the prayer part goes from 7:30 P.M. to 8:30 P.M. The format is simple — we pray the rosary, beginning and ending each decade with a good song, read the Scriptures and have a guest speaker, usually lay, each week. We end the prayer time by joining hands at the Lord's Prayer. Then comes the Sign of Peace. Everyone is invited to give the Sign of Peace to several people they do not know. The rest is history! It's so much fun and it's a winner!

After the prayer session, the Filipino community continues to serenade us with music while we share refreshments at St. Martha's Gazebo. The evening is over by 9:00 P.M. Everyone looks forward to Monday Evening Prayer on the Green each August.

Chapter Fifteen

Evangelizing Is Advertising

Evangelization is nothing more than advertising. Like advertising, it is essential to *sell* a product, no matter how fine the product. I have learned so much from our Protestant sisters and brothers by the quality of their communication. The communications (advertising) must be excellent and of professional quality. People do read and respond to quality advertising. It must be consistent, clear, thought-provoking and attractive to the eye.

Our weekly bulletin at St. Brigid's is nineteen pages (not including the cover and advertising pages). It *costs the parish nothing* and has become a very sought after commodity. People do read it. In addition to pages describing upcoming parish activities and programs, we feature Fr. Richard McBrien's syndicated column along with Androgogy by Fr. George J. Dyer, STD. Fr. McBrien always stirs up a few pots, which is very healthy. On occasion we reprint articles that have appeared in magazines like *America* and *The Catholic World.* The syndicated articles can be reprinted at a very nominal fee and the magazine publishers are very gracious about giving permission to reprint articles. We also print talks that our parishioners have given at special events like World Marriage Day and the Seven Last Words on Good Friday.

Each week I write my own column. Again, people do read it and when I skip a week, I hear about it. I write about what's going on in the parish but I also write a spiritual message that I hope reinforces the homily. The pastor must always be communicating with his people about the events and temporalities of the parish, but he must communicate primarily as the spiritual leader of the community. If he does not do that, he runs the risk of being perceived more as an administrator than as the spiritual leader.

It may seem like a crazy project to produce a bulletin of nineteen pages each week, but there are always so many pages that some have to be eliminated. Once it gets rolling it builds and takes care of itself. Each major ministry produces its own page and does a fine job of it. Thanks to computers and skilled operators they look very professional and well done. Samples of some of our advertising can be found in Part III of this book.

We also advertise in the local papers to reach people who don't come to Sunday Mass. This is a very fine way to evangelize (advertise). It makes the parish more and more visible and accessible to the community. The Lord uses every means and device to reach the hearts of His people. Never underestimate the power and the impact of a welcome extended to the community.

A parish newspaper is also a great tool of advertising. To be really effective it should be available to every household that receives mail — Catholic and otherwise. Yes, there is expense involved, but shouldn't every parish have a budget for evangelization? If we believe in the Lord and in what we are doing, we want to shout it from the roof tops. We should be so proud of our parish family that we want everyone to know about our family.

Parishioners should not just receive mailings pertinent to finances. These are necessary, but sometimes we forget the impact of a letter or mailing that has to do with the faith and life of God's people. Letters to parents about their children's faith lives are very important and well-received. Letters to the engaged, newly married, bereaved, etc. all have the result of bringing into the people's homes a caring and loving Church worth listening to.

Special Seasonal Mailings

We go to great pains at Advent, Christmas, Lent and Easter to send very extensive mailings about the services and opportunities for prayer at these special seasons. It takes a lot of time and preparation to do these, but it pays off. People do come back to church. The mailings are more than informational. They are spiritual and evangelical outreaches of the parish. (The Holy Week Booklet is twelve 8 ½″ x 11″ pages, and can be seen in Part III.)

All of this I realize can be very intimidating, but believe me, once you get it started it takes care of itself. Remember, you shouldn't reinvent the wheel every week or every season. Improve and enhance, yes. Most important, be consistent and strive for excellence. Allow gifted people to become involved and use their gifts. Most of all, be excited about the message and the Lord whom we proclaim.

Enthusiasm is contagious. So is boredom. Does the parish communicate excitement as it prepares for and advertises the upcoming special events? Would you go if you didn't have to?

A Moment With Jesus

Fr. Denis Kelleher introduced me to this winner. I had two phone lines (with new numbers) installed and connected to a special machine that plays a three-minute message of scripture, prayer and encouragement. People can call twenty-four hours a day. I originally intended it for the homebound, but a lot of people like to call up and pray and be prayed for. I change the message a few times during the week. It has improved my personal prayer and daily homilies as I try to say some things from the daily scripture that will help and encourage my dear sisters and brothers.

I think it says volumes about how we care about and love the homebound. There are so many people who find it helpful to hear a friendly voice speaking of Jesus. Jazz it up with a little music and you've done something that will make people's days much brighter — especially your own.

I announced the Moment with Jesus on a special postcard depicting the new Resurrection and Tomb Shrine that was designed for the Easter Season. See, you *can* kill two birds with one stone!

St. Brigid's On-Line

Through the giftedness of Fr. Claude D'Souza and Fr. Tom Costa the parish is now on-line. They are now exploring ways of using the Internet. One of the possible projects is to send E-Mail to all of our college students who are away from home. They are also looking into ways for the parish to reach out to more people and to spread the Word. Again, only our imagination limits our possibilities.

I personally am totally computer illiterate; thankfully, my brothers are not. Everyone doesn't have to know everything, but when people who are gifted and talented are encouraged to use their gifts, wonderful things happen in our parishes.

Chapter Sixteen

The People's Church

St. Brigid's is blessed with an extraordinary staff. We are four priests, two religious sisters, five deacons, a lay staff of two Directors of Religious Education, a Liturgist, a Music Director, a Youth Minister, an Executive Assistant to the Pastor, an Administrator, School Principal and Director of Parish Outreach.

Each staff member is superb in his/her field. We meet, we work together, we struggle and we fight. We also give the parish everything we've got. We serve a community of 5,000 multi-ethnic and multi-racial families. The Lord is blessing us, and wonderful things are happening in the parish. But without the involvement of many people, the staff can do nothing. As I look back on my seven years as pastor of St. Brigid's and ten years as pastor of St. Anthony's in beautiful Rocky Point, one thing is clear: The only things that will work in a parish are the things that people *want* to work and the things the people *make* work.

I am not minimizing the role of the staff, but if it's really going to work, the people have to *own* it and they have to *do* it.

At St. Brigid's there are literally hundreds of people who *own* the Presepio, the CCD, the Outreach, Bingo, the School Board, the Parent's Club, Family Life, the Liturgy Committee, the Thrift Shop, the EM's, the Prayer Groups, the Welcoming Committee, the Bereavement Groups, etc. The Grounds Committee and the Decorating Committee make the church and the green a beautiful place to be.

CYO, Scouts, Pro-Life, Peace and Justice, Finance, Italian

Community, Haitian Community, Spanish Community, Filipino Community, the choirs, RAP Leaders — all of these people have owned their parish. It is theirs. Priests come and go but the people remain. It is *their* parish and they love their parish and they support it. We have just paid off a $1,228,000 indebtedness to the diocese in less than five years. In the new year we will be tithing one tenth of our collections (after our subsidy to the school) to the poor.

When people come to me suggesting a new ministry or activity, I will always throw it back to them with, "Will *you* begin it?" Usually, the answer is "yes" and before you know it a new ministry begins to flower. That's how many wonderful things begin and continue at St. Anthony's and at St. Brigid's.

We aim at every group being led by the people — leaders who have been formed, empowered and trusted. We have to let go of power. When we do so we will never be disappointed as long as we have done our job of formation and continue to support them.

Over the years I've learned that many people know much more than I do and that they can do things better than I can. If I'm not threatened by that, then I can have hundreds of people working with me and I come up looking like a genius! You even get asked to write books like this because people think you know something!

Don't be afraid. Let go and trust. Many years ago in my first parish a great man said to me, "Frank, the more power you give away, the more *real* power you'll have." I can only say to that: Amen!

Part Three
Shout It from the Rooftops

In Part I, I tried to express a theology and spirituality of community building based on the Paschal Mystery. In Part II, I brought you through the year — the Church's and people's — sharing what we have done at different feasts and events to build this family that we all yearn and pray for.

Part III contains samples of advertising which appeared in our bulletin (actual page is 8 ½″ x 11″) and in local papers. The Advent/Christmas, Lent and Holy Week/Easter samples are actual brochures that we mail to all of our parishioners. All these samples are the work of Estelle Peck, who in addition to being Director of Liturgy and Family Life, does our publicity.

Remember, you may have the most wonderful program or event to offer, but if you do not spread the word, who will know about it? We often say, "The people just don't turn out for things." Perhaps the truth is more that we didn't give them a reason to come. We didn't communicate. If you are planning something special in your parish and it isn't preceded by at least four weeks of first class, top notch advertising in your parish bulletin, you are not serious about wanting people to come.

Please help yourself to any or all of these ideas, but then create your own and then write *your* book. Don't try to reinvent the wheel each time. For example, our Holy Week/Easter brochure follows the same basic format each year. We change the particulars and improve the graphics, but we *don't* re-create it every year. This is hard and painstaking work, but well worth the effort. Be patient and build from year to year.

We have the most wonderful product to share — the Lord Jesus Christ. We are doing wonderful things to make Him known. Doesn't He deserve the same kind of creativity that people use to sell a bar of soap? Don't we have an obligation to tell the world about the great things that we are doing in our parishes? Go ahead. You can do it. We did.

Parish of St. Brigid
1995 Advent & Christmas Schedule

Be an Angel!
"Adopt an Angel"
NOEL

In wondrous anticipation of the Christ Child's coming St. Brigid's Parish invites you to participate in our **Angel Tree Gift Program** sponsored by **St. Brigid's Parish Outreach.** On our "Angel Tree," located in the sanctuary of the Church and Our Lady's Chapel, there are angels representing people in our community "waiting" to be adopted for Christmas. Anyone wishing to participate in this program is then invited to purchase a gift for that particular child or adult and bring it to Church on Sunday, December 17.

Come home for Christmas!

Dear Parishioners,

May the Christ Child bring to you and your dear family peace and blessings this Christmas. It is our great joy to welcome you and yours to all the services and opportunities for prayer that the parish offers in this beautiful time of Advent and Christmas.

We again extend a very special welcome to all who have not been very active of late. We welcome you home for Christmas and want you to know how much you are loved by the Lord and his Church.

Finally, you and your loved ones will be remembered in the prayers of the community – especially at all the Masses on Christmas Day.

Again, we wish you a blessed and happy Christmas and a New Year filled with Jesus' choicest blessings.

Merry Christmas!

Fr. Frank Gaeta and Staff of St. Brigid's!

"Would that even today you knew the things that make for peace."

-Luke 19

What kind of presents will be under your tree this Christmas? What kind of toys will you give your children? This Advent the Parish of St. Brigid invites you to seriously reflect on the kind of gifts you will be giving to your family and friends on Christmas. Will they be gifts that show respect for the individual and the earth or gifts that speak of violence? Please watch the parish bulletin for alternative ways to celebrate Christmas and give witness to the sacredness of life.

Find what you're missing!

Daily Mass Schedule in Church

Monday thru Friday:
7:00, 9:00 and 12:10 PM
(The 12:10 PM is followed by confessions)

Saturday:
Mass at 8:30 AM
with Anointing of the Sick

Sunday Mass Schedule

(Please note the adaptations in the regular Sunday schedule for Christmas Eve/Christmas Day.)

Church

Saturday: 5:00 PM; **Sunday:** 6:30; 7:30; 8:45 (Italian); 10:00 (Family); 11:30 AM (Choir); 1:00 & 3:00 PM (Creole)

Our Lady's Chapel in Fr. Sullivan Hall:

Sunday: 9:00; 10:15; 11:30 AM (Spanish); 6:00 PM (Rock/Youth)

Other Opportunities for Prayer

Rosary by Candlelight
Mondays at 8 PM

Charismatic Prayer Meeting
Our Lady's Chapel on Tuesdays at 8 PM; **Exposition of the Blessed Sacrament** on Thursdays from 12:30-5 PM; **Jesus Evenings of Prayer on** First Fridays of the month at 7:30 PM-Liturgy, Praise, Healing;Confessions and Laying on of Hands at 9:00 PM; Nocturnal Adoration from 10:00 PM to 11:00 PM

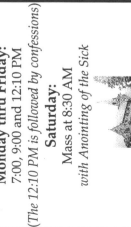

CONFESSION SCHEDULE

The **Sacrament of Reconciliation** is regularly offered Monday thru Friday following the 12:10 PM Mass; First Fridays following the Jesus Evening Mass at 9:00 PM; Saturdays at 6:15 PM to 7:00 PM

Please feel free to call one of the parish priests to make an appointment to receive the Sacrament of Reconciliation at any time.

Friday, December 22 from 7:30 AM to 9:00 PM
CONFESSIONS ALL DAY and EXPOSITION ALL DAY
WITH MEDITATIVE CHRISTMAS MUSIC

7:30 - 9:30 AM	Fr. Frank
9:30 - 11:30 AM	Fr. Claude
11:30 - 12:30 PM	Fr. Augustine
12:30 - 3:00 PM	Fr. Mike & Fr. Tom
3:00 - 5:30 PM	Fr. Frank & Fr. Marty Kirby
5:30 - 7:00 PM	Fr. Frank & Fr. Joe Nagle
7:00 - 9:00 PM	All the priests of the parish in Creole, Español & Italiano

Saturday, December 23

9:30 - 11:00 AM	Fr. Augustine & Fr. Claude
6:00 - 7:00 PM	All the Priests of the Parish in all languages

Holiday Decorating

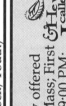

The Decorating Committee invites all parishioners to participate in decorating the Church and Our Lady's Chapel.

Church

Advent Decorating
Thursday, November 30, 7:00 PM

Christmas Decorating
Saturday, December 23, 1:00 - 4:30 PM

Our Lady's Chapel in F.S.H

Advent Decorating
Monday, November 27 at 10:00 AM

Christmas Decorating
Thursday, December 21 at 6:00 PM

All decorations will come down the week of January 9th! The Presepio will remain in the Church until January 27

The Feast Our Lady of Guadalupe

Sunday, December 10

Bi-lingual Mass at 11:30 AM in Our Lady's Chapel; multi-cultural celebration with music, dancing, traditional foods in auditorium following liturgy. Domingo, el 10 de Diciembre, Misa bi-lingüe a las 11:30. Capilla de Nuestra Señora en Sullivan Hall. Recepción Multi-cultural a la 1:00. Aud. en Escuela.

"Fr. Frank Visits With Santa"

Religious Ed. Christmas Party

Tues., Dec. 19 & Wed., Dec. 20

4:15 PM Code Auditorium

~Refreshments
~Gifts for all the Children
~Christmas Carolling

Sixth Annual Children's Christmas Pageant

Sun.~Dec. 3rd~5:30 PM~Church

followed by a pot luck supper in Code Auditorium. There will be a visit from St. Nicholas and treats for all the children!

Rehearsals in the Church:

Mon. Nov. 27th 4:30-5:30 PM

Dress Rehearsal for Entire Cast

Fri. Nov. 30th 4:30-5:30 PM

Masses on the Feast of the Immaculate Conception

Church:

Dec. 7th (Eve) at 5:00 & 7:30 PM
Dec. 8th at 6:30; 7:45; 9:00 AM; 12:10, 5:00 *(Children's Liturgy)* & 7:30 PM.

Our Lady's Chapel:

8:30 PM (Spanish)

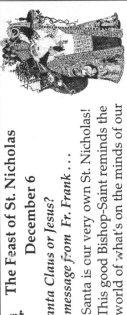

The Feast of St. Nicholas

December 6

Santa Claus or Jesus?

A message from Fr. Frank . . .

Santa is our very own St. Nicholas! This good Bishop-Saint reminds the world of what's on the minds of our children during Advent – Santa Claus and gifts and toys! It also brings us face to face with the conflict of spirituality and commercialism, or Jesus verses Santa. What is the Christian parent to do with the wonder of a child waiting for Santa's visit and the celebration of our Jesus' birth? Use Advent as the gradual journey to Bethlehem . . . bake, decorate your house, set up the Crib, read the many stories of Christmas to your children – spend time together and don't put Santa down! Use him as a shepherd or a wise man at the crib. Santa is yet another believer touched by the Son of God who comes to worship Him !

St. Brigid's /Our Lady of Hope Regional School Christmas Concert

Wed., Dec. 20th, 7:30 PM

Our Lady's Chapel

Give Jesus your heart this Christmas! Fr. Frank extends to all an invitation to spend fifteen minutes in prayer by meditating on the daily readings followed by his personal reflections, in his first book:

"What Shall I Give Him Poor As I Am?"

Reflections for your Advent and Christmastide

Copies of Fr. Frank's book are available at the Schaefer Center.

Procession to Bethlehem Blessing of Outdoor Crib

Sunday~ Dec. 17th
10:00 AM Family Mass

Spanish Posadas

Our Lady's Chapel

Dec. 21~8:00 PM

The Spanish Community will be enacting the Christmas story of Mary and Joseph seeking a birthplace for Jesus.

CHRISTMAS EVE
Sunday, December 24, 1995

Church

Special Children's Liturgies at
4:00 PM & 5:30 PM (*Signed for the Deaf*).
A special friend will pray with us at these Masses and lead our children to adore the BABY JESUS before he goes on his long Christmas Eve journey!

Liturgies in Candlelight
6:45 PM; 8:00 PM; 10:00 PM

Midnight Mass with
Procession with the Christ Child and the Blessing of the Presepio
(*Christmas Carols begin at 11:30 PM*)

Our Lady's Chapel

5:00 PM; 8:00 PM (Spanish);
Midnight Mass with
Procession with the Christ Child and Blessing of Creche

Code Auditorium

Midnight Mass (Creole)

"Glory to God in the highest and peace to all who are on earth."

Merry Christmas

CHRISTMAS DAY
Monday, December 25, 1995

Church

6:30; 7:30; 8:45 (Italian); 10:00 ;
11:30 AM; 1:00 and 3:00 PM (Creole)

Our Lady's Chapel in the School

9:00; 10:15; 11:30 AM (Spanish)

There will be no evening Masses in the Church and no 6:00 Rock Mass in the school on Christmas Day.

NEW YEAR'S DAY
Monday, January 1, 1996
The Solemnity of Mary

Masses in Church Only

6:30; 7:30; 8:45; 10:00;
1:30 AM (Multicultural);
1:00 & 4:00 PM

Please note that there will be no New Year's Day Masses in Our Lady's Chapel.

NEW YEAR'S EVE
Sunday, December 31, 1995

"Peace on earth and good will to all!"

Church

5:00 PM Mass followed by exposition of the Blessed Sacrament from 6:30 PM;
11:00 PM Mass for Peace;
12:00 Midnight Happy New Year Champagne Toast in Rectory

THE EPIPHANY
Sunday, January 7, 1996

The Living Nativity

9:00 Italian Mass

Dopo la S. Messa in Italiano delle 9:00 AM ci sará una processione dei Re Magi e del Presepio Vivente.
Following the 9:00 AM Italian Mass the Living Nativity will accompany the the Three Kings to Bethlehem.

***Family Mass Living Nativity**

1:00 PM January 7

The Christmas Season joyfully comes to a close as we invite all our little ones who were baptized in 1995 to come for a special blessing to the **1:00 PM Mass.** Join the Holy Family and the Living Nativity around the outdoor crib; take pictures of your little ones in the manger; drink hot chocolate and feed the animals!

**The Family Mass will be celebrated at 1:00 PM today*

St. Brigid's Parish celebrates Lent, 1996

Lent Is A Time for Fasting

We always think of the word fasting in connection with Lent. Fasting, by choice or by law, has been part of our Lenten and Christian experience for 2000 years. But why do we fast? What should we be fasting from? We fast to remind ourselves that no "thing" can ever dominate our lives. Our Lenten fast is then a way of restoring right order to our lives. We might also look to fasting as a way of praying. Then our fast becomes a way of saying that the Lord Jesus is more important than any creature. Fasting should restore good health to parts of our spirit that are troubled or sick. Fasting brings us closer to the Jesus who dies so that we might live. We nail to the Cross of Jesus those parts of our hearts that are not yet fully redeemed and do not yet belong to His Kingdom so that we may have new life.Fasting also brings us closer to the poor and the suffering. In our little inconveniences that we call "fasting," we become united with the Christ who is *always* fasting and *always* in pain – His Poor. Fast we must. Everyone must fast from ***hate***, from ***self-concern***, from ***despair***, from ***guilt***, from ***suspicion***, from ***fear***, from ***laziness***, from ***pettiness***. The list is very long of those things that the Lord would have us fast from. Just remember: choose the fast that will make you more loving and more like Jesus otherwise it is a waste of time.

Make Lent '96 a Fast & a Feast you will never forget!

Lent Is A Time for Feasting

We seldom think of the word feasting in connection with Lent, but yet there is no word more appropriate to describe the works of the Holy Spirit in this holy season. It is a time to feast on the goodness and mercy of God and a time to be lavish in sharing these gifts with ourselves and with the world . . . a time to luxuriate in the ***Love of our God.*** It grows into a feast of ***Gratitude*** as our hearts praise the Lord for all the blessings in our lives. We feast on ***Forgiveness*** as we forgive ourselves and all who have hurt us through our lives. Our feasting is filled with ***Compassion*** as we have a new heart for the suffering and pain of the human family. Our feasting gives us a new ***Hope*** as we believe in the goodness of our world and the goodness of people. Our feasting has generous portions of ***Commitment*** as we say our "yes" once again to the Lord. Our feasting is a sharing in the ***Truth.*** We take stands based on truth and conscience and we stick with them. Lent is a great feast of ***Patience.*** We know that growth in ourselves takes time and we therefore accept our frailty and the need to believe in ourselves and others. Finally, our great feast always is finished off by generous doses of the ***Mercy of God*** . . . for this great mercy is our hope for the present and the future. Let us pray for one another as we walk together through the greatest love affair the world has has ever known . . . the life, death and resurrection of our loving Saviour, Jesus Christ.

Ash Wednesday, February 21, 1996

The signing of the cross on your forehead with ashes this Ash Wednesday will be experienced by millions of Christians all over the world. Ashes are a solemn reminder that God is the one in the driver's seat and we are the passengers; that life here on earth is not permanent; that a greater place is being prepared for us. They also remind us that Jesus calls us to change a part of ourselves - not necessarily a change of activities, a change of contracts or even a change of pace, but a change of heart. What do you have your heart set on? Let the ashes you will receive on February 21 be a reminder to set your heart on the kingdom first, "then all things will be given you as well."

Schedule for Distribution of Ashes

7:00 AM Mass & Ashes; 9:00 AM Mass & Ashes;
12:10 PM Mass and Ashes followed by Confessions; 4:30 PM Children's Prayer Service and Ashes; (Ashes will be distributed until 5:30 PM);
7:00 PM Spanish Mass and Ashes; 8:00 PM Mass and Ashes

"Come back to me with all your heart."

Penance or Confession goes far beyond the forgiveness of sin. In this beautiful Sacrament wounds are healed, prejudices are broken down, injustices come to an end, indifferences and misunderstandings are worked out, issues which have been difficult to face are met head on and relationships are renewed. The effects of this sacrament creep into every part of our life experience. Reconciliation can make you whole again and again . St. Brigid's offers many opportunities to celebrate Reconciliation. We encourage you to receive Penance during this Penitential season. If you haven't been to the Sacrament in a long time, now is the time. Come experience healing and peace, come home to Jesus:

Opportunities for Confessions:

Weekdays from Mon. - Fri.: following the 12:10 PM Mass; **Sat.:** 6:15 - 7:00 PM; Following the Jesus Evening. *Also available by appointment.*
Confessions ALL DAY on Wed. of Holy Week, April 3,7:30 AM - 9:00 PM.

Exposition of the Blessed Sacrament

"Come to Him, Rest and Pray"

Our Parish Church is God's dwelling place on earth. The Church is open every day from 6:30 AM to 9:00 PM. Come for some precious and much needed moments of prayer and solace. When you visit the Church we encourage you to inscribe your intentions in the **Book of Remembrance** located by the Blessed Sacrament Altar. In addition, the **Blessed Sacrament** is exposed for adoration each **Thursday following the 12:10 PM Mass until 5:30 PM** and following the Jesus Evenings each **First Friday** of the month.

Tenebrae~ St. Brigid's Wednesday Night Lenten Series 7:30 PM

February 28 — ***Sister Mary Fritz, CSJ***

Director of Bethany House of Prayer and Coordinator of Pax Christi Long Island. Sister will bring us into the desert with Jesus as she examines abuses in our society.

March 6 — ***Father Jim Claffey, CM***

Spent 18 years in rural Panama working with the poor and developing Liberation Theology. Fr. Jim will bring us into the world, thoughts, gifts and spirituality of the poor.

March 13 — ***Sister Chris Mulready, CSJ***

Sister Chris is on the Staff of the Intercommunity Center for Justice and Peace and Chair of Pax Christi Metro. Sister Chris will share her spiritual journey and challenge us to related issues of peace and justice.

March 20 — ***Sister Joan Staudohar, OP***

Sister Joan is Director of Hope Community in Hicksville Long Island, a residence serving the needs of homeless Hispanic women and children. Sister Joan will challenge us to reflect on our own response to the homelessness all around us. Soup Supper at 5:30 PM precedes service.

March 27 — ***Sister Marian Defeis, CSJ***

"I was in prison and you welcomed me." Sr. Marian serves as a Chaplain on Rikers Island and works and writes extensively on justice related issues, in particular on national drug policies and prison reform.

Tenebrae is a Latin word meaning darkness or shadows. In this Prayer Service, adapted from the more traditional praying of the psalms before dawn in years past, we will reflect on the challenging issues which pervade our lives. The one hour prayer service will include congregational and reflective music, scripture readings and the presentation of a guest speaker. The prayer will be enriched by the gradual extinguishing of candlelight signifying the ***apparent*** triumph of evil and failure of God's plan of salvation thus leading us to the joy of Easter and Christ's victory over sin.

Multicultural Way of the Cross

We invite our entire community to follow the Way of the Cross with Jesus. In place of the four Stations of the Cross that took place on Friday evenings in Creole, English, Italian and Spanish in past years, we will have only ***ONE Multi-cultural Stations of the Cross*** using all the languages of the parish. All prayers, readings and music will be printed in Creole, English, Italian and Spanish. While the leader prays a Station in one language, each person present will be invited to participate in their own tongue. Join your entire parish family as we prayerfully accompany the Lord Jesus on his journey to Calvary by participating in this beautiful prayer of the Way of the Cross. The Community comes together to pray the Stations of the Cross on:

****Fridays of Lent***	***3:00 PM***	***Way of the Cross in English***
	8:00 PM to 9:00 PM	***Multicultural Way of the Cross***

Sunday Masses

Church

Saturday: 5:00 PM
Sunday: 6:30 , 7:30 ;
8:45 (Italian);
10:00 (Family);
11:30 AM (Choir);
1:00 ; 3:15 PM (Creole)

Our Lady's Chapel

9:00 ; 10:15 ;
11:30 AM (Spanish)
6:00 PM (Rock/Teen)

Jesus Evenings

Each First Friday St. Brigid's Church fills with God's Holy People bringing their prayers of need, praise and hope to Jesus. This beautiful evening of Charismatic Prayer and Liturgy begins at 7:30 PM in the Church. Join us for the next Jesus Evening on March 1.

Liturgy - Praise - Beautiful Music and Songs - Healing - Confessions - Laying On of Hands Adoration of the Blessed Sacrament

Parent's Club
Dinner & Fashion Show
sponsored by
St. Brigid/Our Lady of Hope Regional School
Thurs., Mar. 7th, 1996
The Milleridge Cottage
Route 106, Jericho
Cocktails at 6:30 to 7:30
Dinner 7:30 to 10:30 PM
Tickets: $30 each*
** available at the School Office or at St. Brigid's Parish Center*

Feast of St. Patrick
Sat., Mar. 16, 1996
8:30 AM Mass ~ Church
Solemn Blessing of Shamrocks
Distribution of Blessed Shamrocks
Sharing of St. Patrick's Faith

Irish Refreshments & Sing-A-Long in St. Anthony's Hall follows Liturgy

A Week of Non-Violence

"Nonviolence is not a garment to be put on and off at will. Its seat is in the heart, and it must be an inseparable part of our every being." *-Gandhi*

The members of the Peace and Justice ministry invite you to enter into a ***Week of Non-Violence*** from ***March 20-26*** ~ a Lenten time of prayer, reflection and action ~ on behalf of all who live with violence in their daily lives, a time for each of us to develop a greater awareness of our own violence toward ourselves, our family and friends, the stranger in our midst or even our environment. The ***Week of Non-Violence*** will begin on ***Wednesday, March 20,*** with a day of fast and special prayer ~ in whatever way you choose. That night, Parish Outreach invites you to a ***Soup Supper*** in ***St. Anthony's Hall*** from ***5:30 -7:30 PM***, a simple meal of bread and soup, a reminder that millions of people in our world go to bed hungry each night. If you wish to help feed the hungry in St. Brigid's Parish, you may leave a donation approximating what you would have spent on dinner that night. Following the Soup Supper we invite you to attend our Wednesday Evening Tenebrae Service at 7:30 PM in church. See this flyer for more information.

The ***Week of Non-Violence*** will continue with activities for children and adults, a special commemoration on ***Sunday, March 24*** of the anniversary of Archbishop Romero's death and will end with an all night vigil in the church on ***Tuesday, March 26***. Please consult upcoming bulletins for more details.

"A society cannot live in peace with itself unless every human person is treated with dignity and all human life is reverenced as sacred." *U.S. Bishops*

Feast of San Giuseppe

Saturday March 16, 1996 6:30 PM Msgr. Code Auditorium
Sponsored by the Italian Community~Come dance and dine!
Tickets: $35 per adult, $15 per child from 5-12. Children under 5 are free.
Sit down dinner to include a wonderful meal, buffet dessert, coffee and espresso. Dinner includes wine and soda.

6th
Annual Children's Passion Play
Sunday Mar. 10
5:30 PM in the Church

A wonderful way to help children learn about the journey of the Cross and Resurrection of Jesus!

The play is a beautifully creative expression of Jesus' journey of the Cross. Beautiful music, song, liturgical dancing, acting, narration and costuming have made this annual event so special for our parish. Children of all ages are invited to participate. Fellowship will follow in Code Auditorium.

Rehearsal Dates (Church):
Thursday, Feb. 29, 5:00-6:00
Monday, Mar. 4, 4:30-5:30
Friday, Mar: 8, 4:30-5:30

Liturgy for San Giuseppe
Tuesday Mar. 19
8:00 PM
Blessing & Distribution of Bread
Fellowship in St. Anthony's Hall
Pasta Fagioli, Italian Dessert and Coffee

The Rules:
U.S. Guidelines for Abstaining and Fasting

During Lent, healthy Catholics age 14 and older are required to abstain from eating meat on ***Ash Wednesday*** and ***every Friday*** during the ***Season of Lent***. On ***Ash Wednesday*** and ***Good Friday*** as well, healthy adult Catholics (age 18-59) are required to ***fast***, limiting food to one full meal with minimal food at the other two meal times and nothing in between. ***Strict observance of the rules of Fasting*** will probably do very little to change our hearts and are in and of themselves not good (except perhaps for our waistlines!) The Church suggests fasting in order to place ourselves in solidarity with the poor, especially with those who suffer from hunger. Perhaps your Lenten fast can mean limiting the excess in your life as is suggested on our Lenten banners you see hanging in the sanctuary. ***Most of all,*** remember that your Lenten tasks are best done with ***joy***. ***Joyfulness*** can be a perfect prayer because it confirms how much we believe in God's love for us.

From Fragmentation To Wholeness

St. Brigid's welcomes well-known and very popular
Fr. Vincent Youngberg, C.P.
of the Passionist Mission Team
Mon., Apr. 15~ Fri., Apr. 19
12:10 & 8:00 PM Mass
St. Brigid's Church

Lent, 1996

Fast from . . .

Discontent *Anger*
Bitterness
Self-Concern
Despair *Guilt*
Suspicion *Laziness*

Feast on . . .

Gratitude *Hope*
Forgiveness *Compassion*
Commitment *Truth*
Patience *The Mercy of God*

From Ashes to Fire
A Companion for Our Forty Days
of
Feasting and Fasting
by
Francis X. Gaeta
Make time for God and yourself!
Spend twenty minutes a day in prayer and you will have a Lent and an Easter you will never forget!

In lieu of the price of the book an offering to St. Brigid's Parish Outreach is requested to assist the poor of our community.

Copies of Fr. Frank's book are available at the Schaefer Parish Center
75 Post Avenue Westbury, NY 11590 334-0021

Prayer for Parents

O God, make me a better parent. Help me to understand my children, to listen patiently to what they have to say and to respond to their questions kindly. Keep me from interrupting and contradicting them. Make me courteous to them as I would have them be to me. Give me the courage to confess my sins against my children and to ask them forgiveness when I know I have done wrong. May I not vainly hurt the feelings of my children. Forbid that I should laugh at their mistakes or resort to shame and ridicule for punishment.

Reduce the meanness in me. May I cease to nag; and when I am out of sorts, help me Lord to hold my tongue. Blind me to the little errors of my children and help me to see the good things they do. Give me a ready word for honest praise. Help me treat my children and those of their own age with respect. Let me not expect from them the judgment of adults. Allow me not to rob them of the opportunity to wait on themselves, to think, to choose, and to make their own decisions.

Forbid that I should ever punish them for selfish satisfaction. May I grant them all their wishes that are reasonable and have the courage always to withhold a privilege that I know will do them harm. Make me fair and just, considerate and companionable, so they will have genuine esteem for me. Help me to be loved and imitated by my children.

O God, give me calm and poise and self-control.

Parish Family Breakfast & Procession with Palms to
St. Brigid/Our Lady of Hope School from the Palm Sunday Family Mass
10:00 AM St. Brigid's Church
March 31, 1996
Full Breakfast will be served in Code Aud.
Holy Week arts and crafts on each table

JESUS HAS DONE IT ALL!
HE IS OUR VICTORY, OUR LIFE,
OUR HOPE, OUR ONLY JOY!

Photo by Al Posillico

~St. Brigid's Parish Easter Sunrise Service at Lido Beach

Parish of St. Brigid
Holy Week and Easter Season
1996

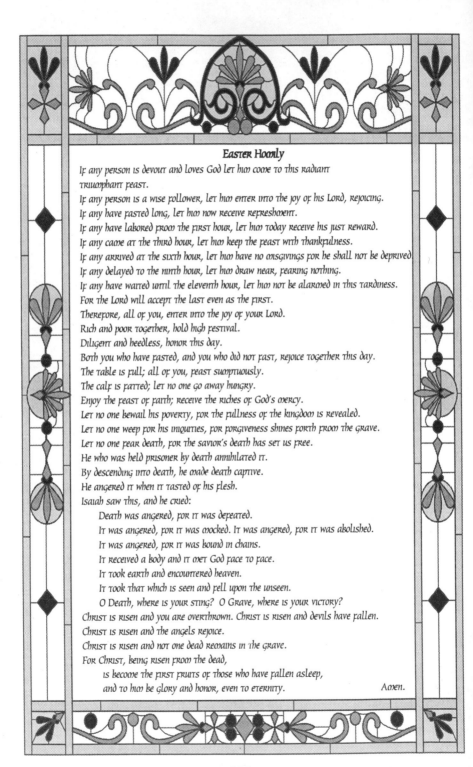

Easter Homily

If any person is devout and loves God let him come to this radiant triumphant feast.
If any person is a wise follower, let him enter into the joy of his Lord, rejoicing.
If any have fasted long, let him now receive refreshment.
If any have labored from the first hour, let him today receive his just reward.
If any came at the third hour, let him keep the feast with thankfulness.
If any arrived at the sixth hour, let him have no misgivings for he shall not be deprived.
If any delayed to the ninth hour, let him draw near, fearing nothing.
If any have waited until the eleventh hour, let him not be alarmed in this tardiness.
For the Lord will accept the last even as the first.
Therefore, all of you, enter into the joy of your Lord.
Rich and poor together, hold high festival.
Diligent and heedless, honor this day.
Both you who have fasted, and you who did not fast, rejoice together this day.
The table is full; all of you, feast sumptuously.
The calf is fatted; let no one go away hungry.
Enjoy the feast of faith; receive the riches of God's mercy.
Let no one bewail his poverty, for the fullness of the kingdom is revealed.
Let no one weep for his iniquities, for forgiveness shines forth from the grave.
Let no one fear death, for the savior's death has set us free.
He who was held prisoner by death annihilated it.
By descending into death, he made death captive.
He angered it when it tasted of his flesh.
Isaiah saw this, and he cried:

> Death was angered, for it was defeated.
> It was angered, for it was mocked. It was angered, for it was abolished.
> It was angered, for it was bound in chains.
> It received a body and it met God face to face.
> It took earth and encountered heaven.
> It took that which is seen and fell upon the unseen.
> O Death, where is your sting? O Grave, where is your victory?

Christ is risen and you are overthrown. Christ is risen and devils have fallen.
Christ is risen and the angels rejoice.
Christ is risen and not one dead remains in the grave.
For Christ, being risen from the dead,
is become the first fruits of those who have fallen asleep,
and to him be glory and honor, even to eternity. Amen.

The Parish of St. Brigid

516-334-0021
75 Post Avenue Westbury, New York 11590

Easter 1996

My dear parishioner:

On behalf of the entire parish staff, I am happy to invite you to share in the touching beauty of Holy Week.

The following pages outline the liturgies and opportunities for prayer that the parish is offering. Although it is not possible to attend every service, it is ***very important that this week truly be "holy."*** *Please make every effort to find time to be with our dear Lord and reflect once again on the love He had for us in laying down His life that we might live.*

It is especially important that our children be allowed to experience the power and beauty of Holy Week. It is very difficult to raise children as Christians in a secular environment. As much as we try to provide worship opportunities that will speak to children, they have little impact ***without the support and faith of mommy and daddy.***

Please share the story of our faith and tradition with your family this Holy Week and Easter. Please bring your children with you to the liturgies and services that you attend.

Pray that during this Holy Week we will all come to a deeper love of Jesus than we have ever known before. Pray that our faith will deepen and that many who have been away from the Lord's Table will come home.

On behalf of all the beautiful men and women of God who minister to God's Holy People, I wish you a Happy and Blessed Easter and I thank them all for making Holy Week and Easter so beautiful at St. Brigid's.

In Jesus' Love,

Fr. Frank Gaeta, Pastor

HOLY WEEK AND EASTER CELEBRATIONS FOR CHILDREN AND FAMILIES

"'Let the children come to me; do not prevent them, for the kingdom of God belongs to such as these.' Then He embraced them and blessed them, placing his hands upon them." *-Mark 10*

Palm Sunday - March 31st -10:00 AM - Family Liturgy, Procession and Family Breakfast On this day all of our families are invited to celebrate the first Palm Sunday. The day will begin at 10:00 AM with the **Family Mass** which will include the distribution and blessing of palms, the proclamation of the Passion and be followed by a procession through the streets of Westbury to the School for a good hearty breakfast. *(See opposite page for more details on breakfast.)* The procession will be accompanied by a marching band from the feasts of Brooklyn. All children are encouraged to wear disciple costumes. *(See page 6 of this booklet for instructions.) Free* tickets to the Breakfast are available at the Religious Education Center or at the Schaefer Parish Center. If you'd like you may park your car behind the school where you can "catch" the free shuttle bus to the church. Your car will then be waiting for you at the school following the breakfast.

Monday - April 1st - 5:30 PM - Passover Seder - Our Lady's Chapel Celebrate a traditional Passover Seder much like Jesus did with His friends at the Last Supper. We will sing psalms, proclaim the Word of God, hear the four questions, learn about ritual foods and feast on a traditional Passover meal complete from matzoh ball soup to nuts! An offering of $5.00 is requested to help defray the cost of the meal. Seating is limited. Tickets may be purchased at the Rel. Ed. Center or the Schaefer Parish Center.

Wednesday - April 3rd - All Day from 7:30 AM to 9:00 PM - the Sacrament of Reconciliation will be celebrated in our church this entire day. Please come with your family to celebrate this beautiful Sacrament of forgiveness and experience the Lord's healing as you prepare to celebrate Easter.

Holy Thursday -April 4th - 10:00 AM- Celebration of the Lord's Last Supper & Washing of the Feet At this beautiful Mass the priests and parents will wash the feet of all the children. We will process with the Blessed Sacrament and then adore the Lord on the main altar. Families are encouraged to spend some time together in prayer before the Blessed Sacrament. Adoration will continue after this celebration until 4:00 PM this day. We have especially arranged this for our young families and Seniors who find it difficult to go out at night. The entire celebration lasts about 1 1/2 hours.

Good Friday - April 5th - 10:00 AM- Veneration of the Cross
At this touching service the children will re-enact the Suffering and Death of Jesus and all will be invited to come forth and hug or touch or kiss the crucifix. It is a very moving sight to see and a beautiful experience to be a part of.

Holy Saturday - April 6th - 9:00 AM. -Blessing of Easter Food
At this brief and simple service we bless food that our people will share at Easter dinner. Come with your family with an item of food for your Easter Table and we will bless it.

Easter Sunday - April 7th -Please come with your entire family to any of the Masses we have scheduled for Easter Day. *(See page 13)*

Sunday - April 21st - 1:00 PM - Special Easter Spring Liturgy and Family Activity Day The regularly scheduled Family Mass will be celebrated at 1:00 PM on this day followed by a party on St. Brigid's Green. Our Easter joy at the Eucharist will continue with pony rides, a ride attraction for children from 18 mos. - 13 years, a visit from Miss "E" Bunny, balloons, hot dogs, pop corn, face painting, etc. Please come and share the joy of this wonderful day!

St. Brigid's Family Breakfast!

When: Palm Sunday

March 31, 1996

Where: Code Auditorium

(in St. Brigid/OLH School, Maple Avenue)

Time: Following the 10:00 AM Family Mass
at St. Brigid's Church

Please join the
Palm Sunday Procession
(weather permitting!)
from the church to the school followed by
our parish family breaking bread together!

FREE tickets can be picked up at the Religious Ed Center or the Schaefer Parish Center!

Park your car behind St Brigid/OLH School before the Mass and take the FREE SHUTTLE BUS to the church so you car will be waiting for your family after breakfast!

PALM SUNDAY MAR. 31, 1996

At each of the Masses the Palms will be blessed and given to God's Holy People as a sign that Jesus Christ is our Savior and King. The Passion is proclaimed at each Mass. Once again we hear the most beautiful love story ever told–God's love for us in Jesus Christ, His Son.

SOLEMN COMMEMORATION OF THE LORD'S PASSION & ENTRANCE INTO JERUSALEM

SATURDAY 5:00 PM Fr. Tom (2 hours)

Solemn Blessing of the Palms on St. Brigid's Green at 4:45 PM

Procession to the Church follows the Blessing Proclamation of the Passion

SUNDAY MASSES

Church:

6:30 AM - Fr. Frank
7:30 AM - Fr. Mike
8:45 AM - Fr. Richard (Italian)
10:00 AM - Fr. Frank (Family)
11:30 AM - Fr. Joe
1:00 PM - Fr. Joe
(Creole) 3:15 PM - Fr. Moise

Our Lady's Chapel in Fr. Sullivan Hall:

9:00 AM - Fr. Claude
10:15 AM - Fr. Richard
11:30 AM - Fr. Tom (Spanish
6:00 PM - Fr. Augustine (Rock)

Holy Rood Cemetery Chapel:

8:00 AM - Fr. Tom
9:30 AM - Fr. Mike
11:00 AM - Fr. Claude

On Palm Sunday and on Easter Sunday we have a special opportunity to remember our beloved deceased.These Masses will be offered for all those buried at Holy Rood Cemetery and all our beloved dead. Come and pray for them in this Holy Place.

Easy no-sew Disciple Costume:

Cut out hole for head. Tie a piece of rope for belt. Shoesor sneakers are fine!

For girls: Cut out second piece of contrasting color for head cover or shawl.

For boys: Cut out rectangular piece long enough to go over shoulders and to knee level.

Palm Sunday Family Celebration
Come as a Disciple!
10:00 AM Family Mass
Fr. Frank

Celebrate the beautiful feast of Palm Sunday & Jesus' Entrance into Jerusalem!

~Family Mass begins at 10:00 AM in the Church

~ Sing "Hosannas" through the streets of Westbury as we process to the School

~ Complete the celebration with a good, hearty breakfast as you break bread with your entire parish family!

SACRAMENT OF RECONCILIATION

CONFESSIONS HEARD ALL DAY ON

WEDNESDAY APRIL 3, 1996

Today, with a prayerful background of recorded sacred music, the Blessed Sacrament is exposed on the Altar. All are invited to come to Church for quiet prayer, adoration and meditation. All are encouraged to receive the Sacrament of Reconciliation today or at any of the other Confession times this week. This is a special time of grace and blessing. If you've been away from the Church for a while, please come back now. Jesus loves you so much and your dear brother priests are so happy to share His mercy and compassion in this Holy Sacrament.

TIME OF CONFESSIONS:	CONFESSOR:
7:30 AM - 9:30 AM	Fr. Frank
9:30 AM -11:30 AM	Fr. Mike
11:30 AM -12:30 PM	Fr. Augustine
12:30 PM - 2:30 PM	Fr. Joe & Fr. Tom
2:30 PM - 3:30 PM	Fr. Claude & Fr. Mike
3:30 PM - 5:00 PM	All the Priests of the Parish in all languages
5:00 PM - 7:00 PM	Fr. Frank & Fr. Joe
7:00 PM - 9:00 PM	All the Priests of the Parish in all languages

"Let us celebrate with a feast, because my son was lost and has been found."

Confessions will also be heard on:

GOOD FRIDAY - APRIL 5, 1996

9:00 PM - After Stations of the Cross

All the Priests of the Parish *(All languages)*

HOLY SATURDAY - APRIL 6, 1996

10:00 AM - 12:00 Noon

Fr. Frank, Fr. Mike & Fr. Augustine *(All languages)*

If it is impossible to get to confession at any of these times, please call BEFORE HOLY WEEK for an appointment for a private confession. (334-0021)

† HOMEBOUND †

If a family member is homebound and unable to get to church, please call the **PARISH OFFICE** (334-0021) so that they may receive the Sacraments at home. It is the sacred **right** of all of our people to be able to receive the sacraments.

HOLY THURSDAY † APRIL 4, 1996

7:00 AM	**Mass and Holy Communion**	**Fr. Claude**
9:00 AM	**Morning Prayer**	**Dcn. Robert P. Broyles**
10:00 AM	**Children's Liturgy** Washing of the Feet - Mandatum Mass of the Lord's Supper Procession with Blessed Sacrament	**Fr. Frank**
8:00 PM	**Mass of the Lord's Supper** (Msgr. Code Auditorium - St. Brigid's/O L H School) The Washing of the Feet - The Mandatum The Procession to the Altar of Repose in the Church	**Fr. Frank (2 Hours)**

An Offering will take place at this Mass for the poor of the Parish.

EXPOSITION OF THE BLESSED SACRAMENT

Following the Children's Liturgy and Procession at 10:00 am the Blessed Sacrament will be exposed on the altar. We have especially arranged this time of Adoration of the Blessed Sacrament for our young families and senior citizens who find it difficult to come out at night. Exposition of the Blessed Sacrament will end with Benediction at 4:00 PM

THE MASS OF THE LORD'S SUPPER

On Holy Thursday Night there will be one Mass of the Lord's Supper celebrated at 8:00 PM in Code Auditorium in the school. This Mass will be a multi-cultural celebration in which all the languages and communities of the Parish Family will come together to express our unity and love in the Lord Jesus and in the Holy Sacrament of the Eucharist. During the Mass, Fr. Frank will wash the feet of twelve members of the community in memory of Jesus' action at the Last Supper. The Washing of the Feet, the Mandatum, is a reminder to all of us that we are called to be a Servant Church washing the feet of one another and the whole world. After Mass we will process with the Blessed Sacrament through the streets of our town to the church on Post Ave. This will be a candlelight procession in which we will honor the Lord in a public way. When we reach the church the Holy Sacrament will be placed on the altar for our people to come and adore the Lord Jesus throughout the night. We invite you to set apart "an hour" to come and watch the Lord.

Bus Transportation: In order to facilitate parking, etc. we invite you to come and park at the church parking lot. Beginning at 6:45 PM a bus will transport people from the church parking lot to the school and will do so until 8:00 PM. When you reach the church at the end of the procession from the school, your car will be there for you to go home. If you DO NOT wish to walk in the procession or do not feel up to it, please feel free to park at the school. At the end of the Mass you may either drive down to the church or go right home

THE WATCH

The Blessed Sacrament will be reserved at the Altar of Repose in church, which will be decorated by our Spanish Community, all through the night until **Good Friday at 6:00 AM.** We invite you to make a commitment to pray before the Blessed Sacrament for an hour from midnight to 6:00 AM. Please call Deacon Phil Matheis at the Parish Center (334-0021) to pledge your hour of prayer before the Blessed Sacrament.

GOOD FRIDAY

APRIL 5, 1996

On Good Friday the Church looks upon the Cross and sees the greatest act of love ever known. Our Savior offers His sacrifice of love upon the Cross. Our parish will offer the opportunity for prayer all day long. Please take time with your children to observe the death of Jesus. Try to make it a day of real mourning, fasting and prayer. Jesus died for you personally. Your name was in His heart as He died. He did it all because He loves you so much. He calls you to love Him in the same way.

9:00 AM	**Morning Prayer**	
10:00 AM	**Children's Liturgy of the Lord's Passion and Death**	**Fr. Joe Nagle**
12:00 Noon to 3:00 PM	**The Three Hour Agony of the Seven Last Words of Jesus on the Cross.** *(Feel free to come to all or part of this service.)*	**"The Saints of Westbury"**

THE THREE HOUR DEVOTION
&
THE SEVEN LAST WORDS
WILL BE PREACHED BY THE
"SAINTS OF WESTBURY"
12:00 Noon to 3:00 PM
(Please feel free to come to all or part of this service.)

Come to the foot of the cross as these "Saints of Westbury" lead you in accompanying Jesus during his final agony. Your love for Jesus will deepen as never before. You will gain new insights as you pray, sing hymns, reflect on holy scripture and meditate on the final words of Jesus as He hung upon the cross. It is you for whom Jesus speaks; it is you for whom He died; it is you whom He loves so much. These beautiful members of our community will inspire you as they share their faith and their love for Jesus.

Good Friday Preachers:

Dorothy & Jim Morris	*"Father, forgive them for they know not what they do.*
Eric Bauman	*"Today you will be with me in paradise."*
Christine Lombardi	*"Woman, behold your Son. She is your mother."*
Linda & Ken Roberts	*"My God, my God, why have you abandoned me."*
Maureen & Frank Pesce	*"I am thirsty."*
Vicki & Richard Russini	*"It is finished."*
Daniel Fisher	*"Father, Father I put my life in Your hands."*

GOOD FRIDAY

3:00 PM — **<u>Our Lady's Chapel in Fr. Sullivan Hall</u>** — **Fr. Tom**
Via Crucis and Spanish Liturgy of the Passion & Death of the Lord Jesus Christ

3:15 PM — **<u>Church</u> (2 Hours)** — **Fr. Mike**
The Solemn Liturgy of the Passion & Death of the Lord Jesus Christ

- Proclamation of St. John's Passion
- Holy Communion
- Veneration of the Cross

5:30 PM — **Stations of the Cross - The Via Dolorosa**
All are invited to be a part of the moving Way of the Cross as we process through the streets of Breezy Hill to the stations as we remember the journey of Jesus to Calvary. Please assemble on St. Brigid's Green at 5:00 PM and be part of this beautiful devotion presented by the Italian Community.

7:00 PM — **Procession with the 'Jesus Sepultado'**
The Fourteenth Station will take place at **Fr. Sullivan Hall.** The Spanish Community will then begin the procession to the church with the statue of the Dead Christ (Jesus Seputaldo). All will follow the statue until it is placed in the church to lie in state until 3:00 PM on Holy Saturday. All are invited to come to church and pray and meditate on the **Passion, Death, and Resurrection of Our Lord.**

8:00 PM — **Stations of the Cross in Church** — **Fr. Mike**
This beautiful and touching **Dramatization of the Stations of the Cross** will be presented by the Young Adult Ministry. **The Young Adults** will lead us through the sufferings of Jesus as we especially remember those victimized by the injustices of our present day world. We will pray for many local and global issues. Let us join our hearts in solidarity with the crucified Lord and with all those who suffer from the sins for which He died.

Good Friday Confessions will follow the Stations at 9:00 PM while Our Lord's Body lies in state.
These confessions will be heard by all the Priests of the Parish - in all languages.

HOLY SATURDAY — APRIL 6, 1996

Today our Church waits by the Tomb. We hope for New Life and Resurrection in Jesus our Lord. We prepare our hearts and minds for the renewal of our Baptismal Promises and the Celebration of the Easter Eucharist.

The Repose of Christ

The statue of the Dead Christ (Jesus Seputaldo) will lie in state in Church until 3:00 PM. All are invited to pray and keep watch as we prepare for the Lord's Resurrection.

9:00 AM — **Morning Prayer and the Blessing of the Easter Food** — **Dcn. Phil Matheis**

We invite our people to bring an item(s)of food that will be eaten at Easter dinner for the Paschal Blessing of the Church upon the sacrament of family life and friendship.

10:00 AM to 12:00 Noon — **Confessions** — **Fr. Mike, Fr. Frank & Fr. Augustine**

3:00 PM — **Final Prayer** (Midday Prayer) — **Fr. Frank**

This prayer service around the Statue of the Dead Christ will be our final prayer before we begin celebrating the Easter Eucharists. We lovingly remove the statue & wait with hope for the Lord's Resurrection.

EASTER MASS SCHEDULE

PLEASE NOTE THAT THERE WILL BE NO MASSES CELEBRATED BEFORE THE EASTER VIGIL ON HOLY SATURDAY.

THE GREAT VIGIL OF EASTER

8:00 PM	Our Lady's Chapel(Spanish)	Fr. Tom
8:00 PM	St. Brigid's Church	Fr. Frank

THE GREAT VIGIL OF EASTER 8:00 PM

CELEBRANT FR. FRANK *(3 Hours)*

We will gather together at 7:45 PM on St. Brigid's Green for the Blessing of the New Fire and the Paschal Candle. We will then follow the Paschal Candle (the symbol of the Risen Christ) into the darkened church spreading among us the Light of Christ.

The Easter Vigil is the most beautiful and most touching Mass of the entire liturgical year. During it, the new members of our families are born again of water and the Holy Spirit. The Easter Vigil is much more than just "Easter Mass." It is the heart of our faith. All the ceremonies and readings are the final preparation for the moment of new birth and life when our brothers and sisters come into the Body of Christ, the Catholic Church. This holy night also prepares the rest of the community for the renewal of the Baptismal Promises and the reception of the Easter Eucharist. The Easter Vigil will not go more than the three hours. Following Mass, coffee will be served on the church steps to welcome our new family members:

Barbara Brown	**George George Costa**	**Kacey Deeb**
John Harris	**Michael Koch**	**Lawrence Simmons**
Melissa Sollowen	**Frances Streit**	**Arthur Tucker**
Jonathan Whitaker	**Jason Whitaker**	**Kristen Wilson**

During the Great Vigil we will . . .

- proclaim the Exsultet
- proclaim the Word of God
- sing the Litany of Saints
- bless the Baptismal font and Easter Water
- celebrate Baptism
- receive new Sisters and Brothers into the Church
- renew Baptismal Vows
- celebrate the Eucharist of Easter

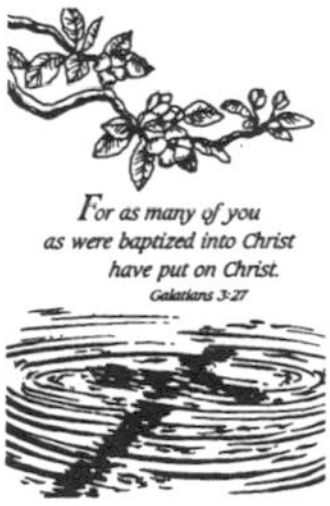
For as many of you
as were baptized into Christ
have put on Christ.
Galatians 3:27

The Lamb of God

Please display the enclosed picture of the **Lamb of God** on your front door during the great FIFTY DAYS of the Easter Season.

... and you were buried with him
in baptism, in which you were also
raised with him through faith ...
Colossians 2:12

Easter Water

Please bring a small bottle to Church and take home some Easter Holy Water. We encourage you to bless your home with this new Easter water.

EASTER SUNDAY
APRIL 7, 1996

Today at Easter Mass, we will be invited to renew our Baptismal Promises and we will be blessed by the sprinkling of the Easter Water. The best renewal of our covenant of love with Jesus is to share in the Easter Sacrament ~Holy Communion. We encourage you to prepare for this New Life by going to Confession during Holy Week.

THE RISEN CHRIST

Please come and venerate the statues of the Risen Christ which will be honored at the Word Altar in the Church and in Our Lady's Chapel.

EASTER MASS SCHEDULE

THERE WILL BE NO MASSES CELEBRATED BEFORE THE EASTER VIGILS ON HOLY SATURDAY

8:00 PM Easter Vigil (Spanish) Our Lady's Chapel
8:00 PM The Great Easter Vigil St. Brigid's Church

EASTER SUNRISE MASS

5:30 AM* Nassau Beach Fr. Mike

The community comes together to celebrate the Holy Eucharist and the mystery of New Life at Sunrise on Easter Morning.

Directions to Nassau Beach:
Take Meadowbrook Parkway south to Exit M-10 - "Loop Parkway." Take Loop Parkway to the end and go right on Lido Blvd. At the second traffic light enter Nassau Beach on the left. Look for signs directing you to St. Brigid's Sunrise Mass.

***Don't forget!!!**
Turn your clocks ahead one hour before you go to bed on Saturday . . . Daylight Savings Time begins this Easter Sunday, April 7.

CHURCH:

6:30 AM Fr. Augustine
7:30 AM Fr. Claude
8:45 AM (Italian) Fr. Tom
10:00 AM Fr. Joe
11:30 AM Fr. Mike
1:00 PM Fr. Claude
3:15 PM (Creole) Fr. Moise
*6:00 PM Fr. Frank

**(Please note: There is NO 6:00 Rock Mass the school. On Easter Sunday, there is a 6:00 PM Mass celebrated in the church.)*

HOLY ROOD CEMETERY :

8:00 AM Fr. Joe
9:30 AM Fr. Frank
11:00 AM Fr. Tom

OUR LADYS' CHAPEL:

9:00 AM Fr. Augustine
10:15 AM Fr. Richard
11:30 AM (Spanish) Fr. Richard

At these Easter Masses we will especially remember our loved ones who are buried in Holy Rood Cemetery and all of our beloved dead.

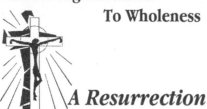

From Fragmentation

To Wholeness

A Resurrection Retreat

St. Brigid's Church

Monday, April 15 to
Friday, April 19
12:10 PM Mass
&
8:00 PM

St. Brigid's welcomes
well-known and very popular

Fr. Vincent Youngberg, C.P.
of the
Passionist Mission Team

"Perfection is unconditional love . . . not being faultless" Integrating his understanding of human development as a result of his education and experience, Fr. Vincent will offer us insight on spiritual growth and the conversion process.

Easter Spring Liturgy & Family Fun Day

Sunday, April 21

1:00 PM St. Brigid's Church

St. Brigid's Parish Seventh Annual Easter Spring Liturgy and Family Day is coming up! We will celebrate the beauty of Easter Life and the joy of the resurrected Jesus at the 1:00 PM Liturgy with all our families and children.

The Easter Liturgy will be followed by:

Pony Rides Face Painting
Refreshments with Hot Dogs, Popcorn,
Chocolate Lollipops and other goodies
and of course, a visit from Miss 'E' Bunny!

St. Brigid Parish

celebrates

Labor Day Sept. 4, 1995
9:00 AM

Good St. Joseph,
pray for us
as we begin another year!

- **Gathering outside and Procession to the Church Portals**
    - Praying of Psalm 122
- **Striking of the Church Portals with the Pastoral Staff**
    - Celebrate new beginnings
    - Opening of the church portals
    - The portals will be opened by couples who are with child, signifying our belief in new life
- **Blessing of the new statue of St. Joseph**
- **Liturgy in honor of St. Joseph the Worker**
- **Liturgy will be followed by:**
    - Drawing of the lucky winners of Summer Maintenance Raffle on St. Brigid Green
    - Drawing for "Dinner for Two" at the Rectory for those who contributed $200 or more to the '95 Bishop's Appeal
    - Labor Day "Salute to America"
    - Breakfast on St. Brigid Green

"I'm going to give it all up and follow St. Francis!"

Blessing of Animals to celebrate the Feast of St. Francis of Assisi

Sunday Oct. 1 2:30 pm St. Brigid Green

Each year on October 4th the Church celebrates the Feast of St. Francis of Assisi, a saint famous for his kindness to animals. In fact, St. Francis was the first person to create the Nativity Scene, using barnyard animals. *(See Ad for St. Brigid's Presepio / Nativity Scene below!).* So that more of our parishioners could join us on this beautiful day of blessing we decided to celebrate it on the **Sunday before** the Feast. So please bring your pets and join us on **October 1st** at **2:30 pm** as we give praise to the Lord for this beautiful earth and the creatures upon it!

Join the Christmas Presepio Team!

Come to the Workers' Meeting!

Monday Oct. 2nd 7:00 pm Church

The St. Brigid's Presepio (Nativity Scene) has become known throughout Long Island and has been visited by literally thousands of visitors. And we anticipate welcoming even larger crowds this year! Anyone who has been involved in this project knows the complexity of the setting up and taking down each year. It takes <u>*many*</u> *loving hours and* <u>*many*</u> *hands. If you can give any time to this project, please come to this meeting and sign up for one of the committees. You don't have to be artistic because there is something for everyone to do. Although we do welcome artists, designers, painters, etc. for those particular areas. The elves have begun setting up the schedules and designing their plans which they will share with you at the meeting on October 2. Hope to see you then!*

P.S. Rumor has it that Fr. Frank brings in Pizza during "work time" to keep the energy level high!

Thanksgiving Day Liturgy

Celebrate the richness of our heritage!

The Parish of St. Brigid will celebrate the beauty and the diversity of its family by coming together to give thankful praise to God for its choicest of blessings . . .

All of God's Holy People in St. Brigid's Parish!

Thanksgiving Day
Multicultural Liturgy
Thursday, November 23, 1995
9:00 am in the Church

Blessing of Thanksgiving Food

We invite you to bring an item of food to be shared at your Thanksgiving Meal that you would like to have blessed.

*The beautiful voices of all the Adult Choirs and Children of the Parish**

We invite all of our children to dress in the costume of their origin. Pilgims & Indians are welcomed!

Distribution of Thanksgiving Day Grace

Thanksgiving Day Grace will be printed in Creole, English, Italian, Spanish and Tagolog.

** Music Rehearsal Schedule for Thanksgiving Day Multi-cultural Liturgy*

All Adult Choirs and Music Ministries of the Parish:

Sunday Nov. 19, 1995 7:00 pm Church

****Attention ~ All Children of the Entire Parish . . .***

We welcome <u>All</u> of our Children to join in singing for this beautiful Thanksgiving Day Liturgy!

Rehearsals will be on:

Wednesday Nov. 22,1995 4:30-5:30 pm Church

No need to call ~ just come to the rehearsals!

Come Home
for
Christmas!

Find what
you're
missing!

We warmly welcome all who come to celebrate the glorious feast of Christmas. We welcome the stranger, the traveler and guest! We welcome our students home from college for a good winter's rest! We welcome parishioners who moved far away but join us today as old friends and guests! We welcome all who have not been active of late in their Catholic faith, and hope they will find new hope and inspiration this Christmas to come back again and again! We welcome our faithful parishioners, loyal and true; may the Lord bless you for all you do! Welcome to all! May our gathering gladden our hearts and deepen our bonds. We are, after all, one People of God redeemed by the light that is Christ. May we walk by the Light and live by the Light, together in love.

MASSES ON CHRISTMAS EVE

Church

Special Children's Liturgies: 4:00 PM and 5:30 PM *(Signed Mass)*.
Santa will adore the BABY JESUS with us before his Christmas Eve journey!
Liturgies in Candlelight: 6:45 PM; 8:00 PM; 10:00 PM
Midnight Mass: Procession with the Christ Child & Blessing of Presepio *(Carols begin at 11:15 PM)*

Our Lady's Chapel in St. Brigid/Our Lady of Hope Regional School

5:00 PM; 8:00 PM *(Spanish)*; **Midnight Mass** with Procession with the Christ Child and Blessing of Creche

Code Auditorium in St. Brigid/Our Lady of Hope Regional School

Midnight Mass *(Creole)*

MASSES ON CHRISTMAS DAY

Church

6:30 AM; 7:30 AM; 8:45 AM *(Italian)*; 10:00 AM; 11:30 AM; 1:00 PM

Our Lady's Chapel in St. Brigid/Our Lady of Hope Regional School

9:00 AM; 10:15 AM; 11:30 AM *(Spanish)*

***No evening** Masses in the Church or in the school on Christmas Day.*

St. Brigid Church
50 Post Avenue
Westbury, New York 11590
516-334-0021

Founded 1850.

"... The Mother Church of all Nassau County."

St. Brigid's Sixth Annual Children's Christmas Pageant

Sunday December 3
5:30 PM
St. Brigid's Church

Children of all Ages!
Be a Shepherd! Be an Angel!
Be a Dancer!

Shepherds and Angels: *No need to sign up. Just come to the rehearsals! Dates cited below.*

Interested in a lead part?
If you are in Second Grade or higher and want a chance to be: ***Mary, Joseph, Innkeeper, A Wise 'Person' (girls or boys), Second Innkeeper, Third Innkeeper*** *or the* ***Angel Gabriel*** *please fill out the form below. Names will be selected by lotto.*

As for the Baby Jesus . . . *if you are* ***6 months old or younger*** *and your mommy and daddy say it's okay, ask them to fill out the form below and submit your name for a chance to be the* ***Infant Jesus.*** *Forms may be submitted either to the Relgious Education Office or to the Schaefer Parish Center by* ***Friday, November 17***. *The drawing will take place on Nov. 19.*

Liturgical Dancers: *If you want to be a liturgical dancer and are in third grade or higher please fill out form below and return by Nov. 17. Someone will get back to you about the rehearsal dates.*

Meeting for All Interested Adults:
If you would like to help out with the pageant come to the meeting on ***Wednesday, November 15*** *at the* ***Schaefer Parish Center***. *There's lots to do . . . costumes, fellowship, sets, narrarators, adult head angels and adult head shepherds, etc. So come on down and lend a hand. It's a great way to get into the Christmas Spirit!*

<u>**Rehearsal Dates for Pageant**</u>:

Monday	***November 20***	***4:30-5:30***	***Church*** *(No Choir practice)*
Monday	***November 27***	***4:30-5:30***	***Church*** *(No Choir practice)*
Thursday	***November 30***	***4:30-5:30***	***Church Dress Rehearsal***

********************************~tear-off~********************************

St. Brigid's Parish Sixth Annual Christmas Pageant

Yes, I want to place my name in the drawing to be one of the ***lead parts*** in the 1995 Christmas Pageant. Please use this form also, if interested in being a ***liturgical dancer.***

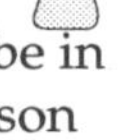

Child's Name: ________________Phone #: ____________ Age: ____

Part(s) desired: ______________________ I understand that I have to be in Second Grade or higher to be Mary, Joseph, an Innkeeper, a Wise Person or the Angel Gabriel. Baby Jesus has to be 6 months or younger!

Please return to the Schaefer Parish Center or the Religious Ed Office by Friday, November 17.

St. Brigid's Parish

Volunteers' Christmas Dance

featuring

The Hal Hoffman 19 Piece Orchestra

Friday December 15, 1995
7:30 PM Liturgy
Our Lady's Chapel

followed by a great

Christmas Party in
Code Auditorium!

Come for dinner, dancing and lots of Christmas cheer with your parish friends and family! Mark your calendar now for this wonderful holiday celebration! If you have volunteered in any capacity, pick up your FREE tickets at the Schaefer Parish Center or the Religious Education Center.

All tickets must be picked up by Wednesday, December 13th!

A Special Invitation for all those baptized in 1995

Sunday, January 7, 1996

1:00 PM Mass

followed by

Procession to Manger with a Living Nativity

Dear very young members of St. Brigid's,

On Sunday, January 7, 1996~the Feast of the Baptism of the Lord, we invite you and all the babies who were baptized in St. Brigid's in the year 1995 to a special blessing at the 1:00 PM Mass. After all, you are the most special members of our family and we would like to see all of you on that day. Please feel free to bring Mommy and Daddy and please don't be embarrassed if they make noise and wiggle. Human beings ~especially big ones ~ have a tendency to do that. They still belong in church and we love them even if they make some noise now and then. I know some kids feel funny when other kids look at their parents because they squirm and make noise. They expect healthy parents to be as dignified and well behaved as little ones! You have to be patient with these kids and tell them: "Hey, adults have just as much right to be in church as kids and babies do!" So please don't be embarrassed by Mommy and Daddy and by all means bring them each Sunday because we want the family to be together where it really belongs ~ in our Father's house.

After the 1:00 PM Family Mass (Family Mass changed to 1:00 that day) we will visit Baby Jesus at the Outdoor Living Nativity and you can take His place in the manger (Daddy will love that for pictures) and just to keep them happy and quiet we will have hot chocolate for them. Hope you can be with us on January 7 and please bring the "Big Ones" along with you.

Love,

Fr. Frank and
All your Sisters & Brothers
at
St. Brigid's

St. Patrick's Day Liturgy

Thursday **9:00 AM Mass**

Come and celebrate the faith of our Parish's heritage and pray for peace in Ireland!

Come and celebrate the faith of Ireland and the beautiful men and women–the first band of immigrants–who came to Westbury in 1850 and began St. Brigid's Parish. On St. Patrick's Day we thank God for our first immigrants and all the succeeding waves of immigrants who have brought faith, love and peace to St. Brigid's.

As we celebrate this magnificent faith of our parish's heritage let us also remember the nearly 3200 men, women and children who have been killed in Northern Ireland during this last quarter century. Let us pray that the weapon of violence will be let go; that peace will be restored and that the senseless suffering of our Irish brothers and sisters will come to an end.

We will also celebrate our great St. Patrick with our annual
Solemn Blessing & Distribution of the Shamrocks
Readings in Gaelic, Beautiful Irish music,
Sharing of St. Patrick's Faith and new Irish jokes from Fr. Frank!
Liturgy will be followed by
Good Irish Refreshments & Sing-A-Long in St. Anthony's Hall!

Come celebrate the

Feast of St. Joseph~San Giuseppe

Saturday March 19
9:00 AM Liturgy
St. Brigid's Church

St. Joseph was, of course, the spouse and protector of Mary and foster-father of the Holy Child. He was a carpenter, a hard-working small businessman, a craftsman, a man who bore the heavy responsibility of provider and leader of the family. He is the special guardian of families everywhere, a patron for hard-pressed modern fathers, a man whose role shows the importance and honor which the Christian Church attaches to fatherhood and family life.

Mass, Blessing & Distribution of Bread followed by Fellowship with Italian Pastries and Zeppole

The figure of St. Joseph sheds light and warmth onto this sometimes difficult world. We see here a father who had a unique dignity but did not presume it; a man of integrity and honor - a just man. It was him whom Our Lord would have as a model for manhood - who taught Him the basic skills which earned the family income, he who presided over family worship, discussions, excursions and festivities. In Italy, March 19th is a day on which fathers are especially honored. The traditional food for St. Joseph's Day is donuts or *zeppole* and *pasta con Sarde (See recipe enclosed in this bulletin!)*

There is also a strong tradition which believes that St. Joseph is invoked by girls seeking a good husband!! Because St. Joseph was not a young man when he was espoused, he is said to be of help to women who are *getting beyond* a marriageable age! Finally, because he was a carpenter, it is said, that he will give you a marvelous husband but also a "knock on the head" - some little, or large, inconvenience attached to your marriage -just to remind you that you can't expect everything to be perfect this side of heaven!!

Come and break bread with your entire Parish Family on St. Joseph's Day - Saturday, March 19th, 9:00 AM Mass

St. Brigid's Baby Shower

Mother's Day, Sunday, May 12

Gifts will be accepted at all weekend Masses!

St. Brigid's Parish Outreach and Family Life Ministry invite the Parish Family of St. Brigid's to participate in a ***BABY SHOWER*** *on* ***Mother's Day, May 12, 1996.***
As a way to recognize and to celebrate the gifts of life and love that each of us has received from our mother, we invite you to respond to the needs of the mothers in our community who are unable to provide for their babies.
We have listed the most basic layette items needed by new mothers and invite you to present your gift at the Altar of the Lord. A bassinet will be placed in the sanctuary of the Church and Our Lady's Chapel which we hope will be filled with your gifts for the newest members of our global community. May God bless you for your love and generosity.

Suggested Baby's Basic Layette Items

Please . . . only NEW items and do not wrap!

Snap-side Shirts (size 3, 6, 12 months)
Slip-on Undershirts (size 6 mos - 3 years)
One-piece Creepers (size 6, 12, 18 months)
Drawstring Gowns (size 6 - 24 months)
Kimonos (Size 6-24 months)
Acrylic Sweaters - Bonnets- Booties Sets
Diapers - cloth or "disposables"
Terry-hooded Towels and Wash Cloths
Cotton Receiving Blankets
Washable Crib Blankets
Fitted Crib Sheets, Waterproof Sheets
Quilted Pads, Baby Wipes
Vaseline, Diaper Ointment
Plastic Baby Bottles
Baby Shampoo, Lotion, Baby Oil
Nail Scissors, Infant Socks, Rattles, Pacifiers, Feeding Spoons,
Plastic Feeding Set, Bibs,
Handmade Knitted and Crotcheted Items greatly appreciated!

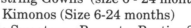

Feast of Corpus Christi

Saturday June 17th, 1995 5:00 PM Mass

Join the entire
Parish Family of St. Brigid's
on the beautiful
Feast of the Body and Blood of Christ
We will offer praise and adoration
to our Lord Jesus Christ in
Liturgy, Procession, Benediction & Fellowship

Multicultural Celebration of the Eucharist in Church at 5:00 PM.

Eucharistic Procession will follow the Multi-cultural Mass through the surrounding streets of the church and school neighborhoods.

Benediction of the Blessed Sacrament

Benedictions will be celebrated at several "chapels" along the way in Italian, Filipino, Creole, Spanish and English. We will end our procession with a final Benediction on St. Brigid's Green in English.

Fellowship to follow on St. Brigid's Green

Mass will end promptly at 6:00 PM with the procession beginning immediately. We will then march the 1.6 mile route stopping for each Benediction along the way. Our celebration will end as always . . . *from Holy Hour to Happy Hour* . . . with fellowship on the lawn.

Please come in comfortable clothing!
Wear your walking shoes! Bring the kids!
All societies are encouraged to carry their banners.
Everyone will receive a flower graciously being made and designed by the Filipino Community and the Corpus Christi Committee. We ask that each person bring flower petals from their gardens so that we can "carpet" the procession route for the Blessed Lord.

If you would like to help in any way with the preparations please call Estelle at 334-0021.

This is a beautiful moment in our Parish Life to not only give adoration and praise to the Lord Jesus in the Holy Sacrament but to thank the Lord for the gift of one another and all the colors, cultures, languages and races which make up the Body of Christ in "Wonderful Westbury."

SAINT BRIGID ON LINE

Yes, It's true!
St. Brigid's is finally joining
the electronic communication age!

We just got a modem
and we're ready to get your e-mail.
We are compiling e-mail directories.
If you have an e-mail address, let us know it
by e-mail direct to the Church
and we will begin to put together
a Parish e-mail directory.

Can you just imagine what Fr. Frank
will be sending out by e-mail?
It's almost frightening!

We also want the e-mail addresses
of all of our young people who are away at school.
We will then be able to keep in touch with them
and let them know what's happening
and what may be planned for vacation time.
It's just a start-but we're excited about it,
and are always open to offers of help!
Your "e-mailmen" are Father Tom and Father Claude
We're still trying to show Fr. Frank
where the on/off switch is!

St. Brigid's Family: e-mail StBrigidPa@aol.com
Fr. Tom Costa: e-mail ThomRev@aol.com
Fr. Claude D'Souza: e-mail ClaudeDS@aol.com

Royalties from this book will go to fund
ST. BRIGID'S WELL
Fr. Fred Schaefer Memorial
Satellite of St. Brigid's Parish Outreach
in New Cassel
Westbury, New York

Published by Resurrection Press

A Rachel Rosary	*Larry Kupferman*	$3.95
Catholic Is Wonderful	*Mitch Finley*	$4.95
Common Bushes	*Kieran Kay*	$8.95
Christian Marriage	*John & Therese Boucher*	$3.95
Discovering Your Light	*Margaret O'Brien*	$6.95
The Gift of the Dove	*Joan M. Jones, PCPA*	$3.95
Healing through the Mass	*Robert DeGrandis, SSJ*	$7.95
Healing the Wounds of Emotional Abuse	*Nancy Benvenga*	$6.95
Healing Your Grief	*Ruthann Williams, OP*	$7.95
His Healing Touch	*Michael Buckley*	$7.95
Let's Talk	*James P. Lisante*	$7.95
A Celebration of Life	*Anthony Padovano*	$7.95
Heart Business	*Dolores Torrell*	$6.95
A Path to Hope	*John Dillon*	$6.95
Inwords	*Mary Kraemer, OSF*	$4.50
The Healing of the Religious Life	*Faricy/Blackborow*	$6.95
The Joy of Being a Catechist	*Gloria Durka*	$4.50
Transformed by Love	*Margaret Magdalen, CSMV*	$5.95
RVC Liturgical Series: The Liturgy of the Hours		$3.95
The Lector's Ministry		$3.95
Behold the Man	*Judy Marley, SFO*	$3.50
In the Power of the Spirit	*Kevin Ranaghan*	$6.95
Young People and... You Know What	*William O'Malley*	$3.50
Lights in the Darkness	*Ave Clark, O.P.*	$8.95
Practicing the Prayer of Presence	*van Kaam/Muto*	$7.95
5-Minute Miracles	*Linda Schubert*	$3.95
Nothing but Love	*Robert Lauder*	$3.95
Faith Means... If You Pray for Rain, Bring an Umbrella	*Antoinette Bosco*	$3.50
Stress and the Search for Happiness	*van Kaam/Muto*	$3.95
Harnessing Stress	*van Kaam/Muto*	$3.95
Healthy and Holy under Stress	*van Kaam/Muto*	$3.95
Season of New Beginnings	*Mitch Finley*	$4.50
Season of Promises	*Mitch Finley*	$4.50
Stay with Us	*John Mullin, SJ*	$3.95
Still Riding the Wind	*George Montague*	$7.95

Spirit-Life Audiocassette Collection

Hail Virgin Mother	*Robert Lauder*	$8.95
Praying on Your Feet	*Robert Lauder*	$8.95
Annulment: Healing-Hope-New Life	*Thomas Molloy*	$8.95
Life After Divorce	*Tom Hartman*	$8.95
Path to Hope	*John Dillon*	$8.95
Thank You Lord!	*McGuire/DeAngelis*	$9.95
Spirit Songs	*Jerry DeAngelis*	$9.95
Through It All	*Jerry DeAngelis*	$9.95